COOKBOOK

BPI INDIA PVT LTD

SHINE GROUP © 2011 Shine Limited.

Shine, MasterChef and the MasterChef logo are trademarks of Shine Limited and used under license. All Rights Reserved.

Based on a format by Franc Roddam. In association with Ziji Productions.

ISBN: 978818497397-6

Food styling and photography by Saba Gaziyani

© BPI INDIA PVT LTD, 2011

Published by

BPI INDIA PVT LTD
F-213/A, Ground Floor, Old Mehrauli Badarpur Road,
Lado Sarai, New Delhi- 110030 (India)
Tel: +91-11-43394300-99
e-mail: sales@bpiindia.com

 SHINE GROUP

 StarPlus
Rishta Wahi, Soch Nayi

 MasterChef INDIA

 BPI INDIA PVT LTD

Licensing Partner
DREAM THEATRE PVT. LTD

StarPlus

Rishta Wahi, Soch Nayi

Star Plus, India's leading Hindi entertainment channel, has inspired imaginations across the length and breadth of this country with amazing content, stories and ideas. Its new identity, the Ruby Star, reflects the channel's new philosophy and thinking, by which content and programming echo a fresh perspective on life and relationships.

And this new way of thinking has given birth to new ideas. A show like MasterChef India is testament to this transformation, giving an opportunity to thousands to follow their dreams.

MasterChef is a competition that allows amateur cooks to demonstrate their culinary prowess. It is a nationwide quest to find the best amateur cook in the country: someone whose passion, skill, imagination and love for food can create extraordinary gastronomic experiences.

The show provides a once-in-a-lifetime opportunity for home cooks to step into the limelight and taste success. It is an arena in which those who cook as a hobby are put to the test and judged by world-renowned chefs. And more importantly, contestants get the invaluable experience of working under the tutelage of the most celebrated chefs in the country.

And as they compete head-to-head with each other, the contestant whose talent, creativity and skills impress the judges the most is invested with the title of MasterChef India.

Pankaj Bhadouria, the first winner of MasterChef India, is from Lucknow. She resigned from her job as a school teacher to become a part of the MasterChef India Kitchen. And today, as India's 1st MasterChef, she continues to enthrall the nation with her extraordinary culinary skills. Her unique recipes for quick-fix dishes that can be made in 30 minutes, gourmet meals, delectable desserts, as well as those she showcased in the MasterChef Kitchen, have been included in this cookbook, so you can create them in your own kitchen. Recipes by the two celebrated judges Chefs Kunal Kapoor and Ajay Chopra, and some star recipes from other contestants in the competition have also been included in the book.

Enjoy the MasterChef India Cookbook, relive some of the most exciting moments of the competition and create wonders...create magic!

CONTENTS

FOREWORD

Tasty Dish Varna Game Finish!

MasterChef India is a first of its kind national quest which crowns the best amateur cook in India as MasterChef.

It is not only a TV show but a phenomenon which has enthralled the imagination of the entire nation: a reality show featuring extreme competition where the finest amateur culinary talents are put to the test.

We don't eat food just to fill our stomachs, but to satisfy our souls. They say one's personality and mood are reflected in one's food choices. MasterChef recognises the deep emotional connection between the food we eat and our innermost being. Therefore, the show is not only about the creation of exciting and innovative dishes, but the roller-coaster of emotions that the participants experience in a competitive environment: pride, dignity, passion, pressure, disappointment, frustration, but above all joy!

I hugely enjoyed my role as a judge in the MasterChef Kitchen, critiquing the dishes created by the 12 best amateur chefs in the country. Their competitive spirit and passion were there for all to see, as they fought vigorously for the title, with Pankaj finally emerging as the winner.

And now, I am proud to present to you The MasterChef Cookbook, filled with delightfully innovative recipes created by India's first MasterChef – Pankaj Bhadouria.

My two co-judges - Chef Ajay Chopra and Chef Kunal Kapoor - have contributed some recipes from their vast repertoire as well. The book also contains exciting recipes created by contestants in the MasterChef Kitchen.

Do try out these unique recipes which have been selected and compiled just for you. I can guarantee they will bring you as much pleasure and excitement as I experienced in the company of the talented and creative participants of MasterChef India Season One!

Bon appétit!

—Akshay Kumar

CHEF KUNAL KAPOOR

Chef Kunal Kapoor is the Executive Sous Chef at Leela Kempinski, Gurgaon. He is also the proud chef of DIYA, the speciality Indian restaurant, which has won the title of Best Indian Restaurant in Gurgaon twice in a row, and is rated amongst the top 5 Indian restaurants in Delhi and Delhi NCR. Other restaurants that have won him awards are Made in India at Radisson Hotel, Noida, Delhi, and Dhaba at the Claridges, New Delhi.

Chef Kunal graduated from the Institute of Hotel Management, Chandigarh and started his career at the Taj group of hotels. His culinary knowledge and experience is vast and encompasses both Indian and international cuisines. However, he has a special gift for preparing Indian curries and kebabs, which prompted Mr. Jiggs Kalra, the doyen of Indian cuisine, to declare him the "next big guy in kebabs and curries in India".

A winner of many culinary awards and titles in his decade-long career, he was listed as one of the Best Chefs in India by India Today magazine, named Gourmet Guru by Food & Nightlife magazine, and recently honoured as one of the Top 20 Chefs of India.

CHEF AJAY CHOPRA

Chef Ajay Chopra is the Executive Chef at The Westin Mumbai Garden City.

He began his culinary career with the Cecil, Oberoi Hotel in Shimla, and went on to complete a management training program at the Oberoi Center for Learning and Development (OCLD). Since then, Ajay has achieved success after success. He was the chef of Lotus Café, the busiest coffee shop in Mumbai, which bagged the Times Food Guide Award for the best coffee shop. He then took over the reins of Saffron, the speciality Indian restaurant to which celebrities and critics flocked.

Having reached great culinary heights in Mumbai, Chef Ajay moved to London to become the Executive Head Chef of the Mint Leaf chain of restaurants. In two short years, Ajay was named one of the 8 best Indian chefs in London. After a two-and-a-half-year impactful stint in London, he returned to India as Executive Chef of the Goa Marriott Resort. He now heads a team of 120 professionals at the Westin Mumbai, and is committed to taking the restaurants at the Westin to greater heights by treating guests to memorable gastronomical experiences.

Pankaj Bhadouria - Winner of MasterChef India Season One

My tryst with food began at the age of 12, thanks to my parents who were excellent cooks themselves. I inherited from them a love for food, which has always been a source of great joy. Much as I took cooking seriously, and much as my family and friends enjoyed the fruits of my experiments in the kitchen, I considered cooking a hobby, an activity to pursue purely for pleasure, never as a career.

When I set out to earn a living, I turned to one of the noblest of all professions - teaching. I spent 16 fruitful and enjoyable years teaching English at the secondary level, before I quit my job to finally pursue my true passion - cooking. When the opportunity to participate in MasterChef appeared, I was presented with a life-changing choice: continue in a satisfying career, or take the plunge, throw caution to the wind and follow my passion. I reasoned that opportunity knocks at one's door but once, so if I played safe and quit the show, I might regret having missed the one chance life was offering me. I opted to take the risk, quit my job and give it a go. To my surprise, I was encouraged by my family, who is my greatest source of inspiration and support.

My Journey in MasterChef India

From an amateur cook to MasterChef India, the journey has been amazing!

It all started with a simple SMS and then a phone call. Then the Lucknow auditions and finally a call to participate in the Mumbai auditions. My 'Drums of Heaven with Stir-fried Veggies in a Fried Noodle Basket' earned me a place in the top 40. From there to Karjat for the Boot Camp was a journey filled with loads of apprehension, having quit a stable job to follow my heart. I could not know whether I would finally make it to the top 12 or not, yet I had taken the biggest risk of my life!

Win, I did - despite my own apprehensions, the many hurdles I had to overcome, and the high standards of the judges. I finally achieved what I aspired for and was one of the top 12 contestants of MasterChef India!

Thanks to my unswerving faith in the Almighty, I was never afraid of what awaited me. I knew that if this was where He had steered me, this was the course He had charted for me in my life. And with this belief, I started my journey in the MasterChef Kitchen.

Each task in the MasterChef Kitchen brought before us a new challenge which got tougher and tougher with each passing day. The MYSTERY BOX challenge had Bhoot Jholokia, the most fiery chilli in the world along with other ingredients which made the strangest combination. The first TEAM TASK had a strong set of individuals working together who failed to come together as a team. The lesson was well learnt and the DHABA TASK turned into a brilliant victory. Cooking for the first family of Bollywood - the Kapoors; the honour of cooking for the Maharana of Udaipur; the emotionally charged moments where we met our families; the one time that I wore the black apron as I fought for my survival with an injured elbow; Chef Rohit Gambhir's words of appreciation; pairing with Joe to become the first semi-finalists, then becoming the first finalist of the show and the first one to move to the top two; Chef Avijit Ghosh's approval; the highly appreciative comments of the judges when I presented my final dish of the show – each day, each task, each moment will remain etched in my memory forever.

And now the fulfillment of another dream – to have a cookbook published. For years I pored over recipes in magazines and books, making notes and putting my own spin on traditional Indian and international foods. My greatest satisfaction comes from finding local alternatives to ingredients which are not easily available, thus enabling me to reproduce dishes that call for unusual or foreign ingredients. I was further

encouraged by my family and friends: every time I cooked something special, one or other appreciative guest would urge me to share the recipe.

This, then, is the answer to those requests, and I am proud and happy to offer this collection of my favourite recipes from the competition, and my own repertoire of tried and tested recipes that I have built over the years.

—Pankaj Bhadouria

For my wonderful family

Mom-in-law Kusum Lata Bhadouria - thanks for always being there; my soulmate, my better half - Charu; the light of my eyes, my kids - Sonalika and Siddhant.

Photographs by Manish Nirwal

Quick-Fix

This is a good way to get veggies into reluctant kids! A perfect winter warmer that contains all the nutrients necessary for growing children.

SUBZ SHORBA

Hearty Vegetable Soup

Pankaj Bhadouria

Preparation Time: 10 minutes
Cooking Time: 20 minutes
Serves: 4

Ingredients

Butter	2 tbsp
Onions, diced	2 large
Potatoes, diced	2 large
Carrots, diced	2 large
French beans, diced	10
Cabbage, shredded	100 g
Bay leaf	1
Cinnamon	1-inch stick
Tomato purée	1 cup
Black pepper powder	1 tsp
Roasted cumin powder	½ tsp
Salt to taste	

To garnish

Chopped coriander leaves	1 tbsp

To serve

Crusty bread or toast

Method

- Heat the butter in a pan. Add the onions and sauté till soft.

- Add all the vegetables along with the bay leaf, cinnamon stick and 2½ cups water. Cook till the vegetables are soft. Or pressure-cook for 6-8 minutes. Remove from the heat and set aside to cool. Strain and reserve the stock.

- Purée the cooked vegetables in a blender. Pass the purée through a sieve.

- Pour the vegetable purée, reserved stock and tomato purée into a pan. Bring to a boil, reduce the heat and simmer for 10 minutes.

- Season with the pepper, roasted cumin powder and salt. If the consistency is too thick, thin it down with some water.

To serve: Pour the soup into bowls and garnish with the chopped coriander leaves. Serve with crusty bread or toast.

MINTY GREEN PEA SOUP

Pankaj Bhadouria

Preparation Time: 5 minutes
Cooking Time: 20 minutes
Serves: 4

Ingredients

Butter	2 tbsp
Onion, finely chopped	1 medium
Garlic, finely chopped	2 cloves
Shelled peas	2 cups
Mint leaves	1 cup
Vegetable stock	2½ cups
Salt	¼ tsp
Black pepper powder	¼ tsp
Cream	1 cup

To garnish

Cream	3 tbsp

To serve

Crusty fresh bread or breadsticks

Method

- Heat the butter in a large pan; add the chopped onion and cook on a low heat for 2 minutes, or until the onion is soft but not brown. Add the garlic and cook for a minute.

- Add the peas, chopped mint leaves, and three quarters of the stock. Bring to a boil, lower the heat to medium and cook, covered, for 20 minutes.

- Process the soup in a blender to make a thick purée.

- Return the purée to the pan, season with salt and pepper, and stir in the rest of the stock and the cream. Simmer for a few minutes.

To serve: Ladle the soup into bowls and swirl some cream over the top. Serve with crusty bread or breadsticks.

14

This is an all-time favourite at my home and particularly refreshing in summer.

Pancakes are a favourite with my kids and so is chocolate sauce. Served together, they are the stuff dreams are made of! The orange coulis adds the X Factor to an already delicious dessert.

PANCAKES WITH CHOCOLATE SAUCE AND ORANGE COULIS

Pankaj Bhadouria

Preparation Time: 10 minutes
Cooking Time: 20 minutes
Serves: 6

Ingredients

Pancakes

Refined flour (*maida*)	250 g
Eggs	2 large
Milk	1⅓ cups
Sugar	100 g
Baking powder	1 tsp
Vanilla essence	1 tsp
Vegetable oil	3 tbsp

Chocolate sauce

Low-fat fresh or packaged cream	1 cup
Plain chocolate	200 g
Unsalted butter	1½ tbsp

Orange coulis

Orange juice	2 cups
Sugar	½ cup

Method

- For the pancakes, mix all the ingredients together with 1 tablespoon of oil and whisk well. Do not use a food processor as the pancakes will turn rubbery. Leave the batter to stand for 5 minutes.

- Lightly grease a frying pan with oil. Stir the batter before making each pancake. Pour a ladleful of batter into the pan. Do not spread the batter.

- Cook for about 1½ minutes till bubbles begin to appear on the surface and the underside begins to brown. Flip the pancake over and cook for another minute. Remove to a plate.

- For the chocolate sauce, whisk all the ingredients in a saucepan over a gentle heat till the chocolate melts.

- For the orange coulis, whisk the orange juice and sugar together in a pan. Bring to a boil and cook till the mixture thickens to a one-string consistency.

- Swirl the pancake a few times in the coulis.

To serve: Stack the orange coulis-soaked pancakes one on top of the other and drizzle with the chocolate sauce.

QUICK PEPPER CHICKEN WITH GREEN SALAD

Pankaj Bhadouria

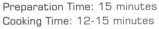

Preparation Time: 15 minutes
Cooking Time: 12-15 minutes
Serves: 4

Pepper Chicken

Ingredients

Boneless, skinless chicken breasts	500 g
Lemon juice	2 tsp
Crushed black peppercorns	3 tsp
Ginger paste	2 tbsp
Garlic paste	2 tbsp
Vegetable oil	3 tbsp
Cream	3 tbsp
Salt	½ tsp

To garnish
Crushed black peppercorns

Method

- Wash the chicken, pat dry and cut into cubes.
- Marinate the chicken in a mixture of the lemon juice, crushed pepper, and ginger and garlic pastes for 10-12 minutes.
- Baste with oil and cook under a hot grill for 3-4 minutes. Turn and baste again and grill for 2 minutes. Collect the dripping juices in a tray placed underneath the grill.
- Put the chicken into a pan with the collected juices, the cream and salt, and cook for another 3-4 minutes. Be careful not to overcook the chicken or it will dry out. Remove from the heat.

Green Salad

Ingredients

Green capsicum, diced	1 small
American corn kernels, blanched	3 tbsp
Iceberg lettuce, shredded	1 large head
Olive oil	2 tbsp
Salt	¼ tsp

Method

- In a bowl, toss the diced capsicum, blanched corn and shredded lettuce with the olive oil and salt. Place in a refrigerator to chill. Serve cold.

To serve: Arrange the salad on a platter and place the chicken on top. Sprinkle with crushed peppercorns.

A deliciously quick option for an evening meal for the whole family.

Rice nachos? Actually, this was something
I came up with on the very first task in the
MasterChef kitchen. Jazz the nachos up with a
tangy salsa for a lip-smacking snack.

CHILLI RICE NACHOS AND ROASTED TOMATO-PEPPER SALSA

Pankaj Bhadouria

Preparation Time: 5 minutes
Cooking Time: 25 minutes
Serves: 4

Ingredients

Chilli rice nachos

Rice flour	200 g
Unrefined maize flour (*makai ka atta*)	50 g
Salt	1 tsp
Dried chilli flakes	1 tsp
Butter	3 tbsp
Vegetable oil for deep-frying	1 cup

Roasted tomato pepper salsa

Red peppers (capsicums)	2
Green peppers (capsicums)	2
Tomatoes	2 large
Garlic, finely chopped	6 cloves
Onion, finely chopped	1 large
Pitted olives, finely chopped	1 tbsp
Salt	½ tsp
Vinegar	2 tbsp

Method

For the nachos

- Mix the rice flour and the maize flour together in a bowl or large platter. Add the salt and chilli flakes and mix well.

- Add the butter and knead with a little warm water to make a stiff dough. Set aside, covered, for 10 minutes.

- Divide the dough into 12 parts. Roll each part into a ball. Roll out into an 8-inch disc. Prick with a fork to prevent it from puffing up.

- Place on a moderately hot *tawa* and cook on both sides for 2 minutes, or till done. Cool the discs and cut each one into 8 triangles.

- Heat the oil in a *kadai*. Slide the triangles into the moderately hot oil and fry till golden. Remove with a slotted spoon and drain on absorbent paper.

For the salsa

- Grill the whole peppers and tomatoes for 15 minutes, or till black on the outside but not burnt. Peel the tomatoes and peppers and chop fine. Transfer to a bowl.

- Add the chopped garlic, onions and olives, salt, vinegar and the remaining chilli flakes. Mix well.

To serve: Arrange the nachos on a platter and serve with the salsa.

POSTO CHINGRI WITH LUCHI

Sesame and Poppy Seed Prawns with Deep-fried Puffed Bread

Pankaj Bhadouria

Preparation Time: 25 minutes
Cooking Time: 15 minutes
Serves: 4

Ingredients

Small prawns	450 g
Ginger paste	1 tbsp
Lemon juice	2 tbsp
Turmeric powder	½ tsp
Salt	1 tsp
Sugar	½ tsp
Black sesame seeds	1 tbsp
Poppy seeds (*khus khus*)	2 tbsp
Vegetable oil	3 tsp
Onion seeds (*kalonji*)	¼ tsp
Red chilli flakes	1 tsp
Finely chopped green chilli	1 tsp

To serve
Fresh green chillies

Method

- Wash, peel and devein the prawns.
- Marinate the prawns in a mixture of the ginger paste, lemon juice, turmeric powder, salt and sugar for 10 minutes.
- Dry-roast the sesame seeds in a pan on low heat until toasted and fragrant. Set aside.
- Grind the poppy seeds with a little water to a paste.
- Heat the oil in a pan; add the onion seeds and sauté for a few seconds. Add the marinated prawns and sauté for 2 minutes. Add the poppy seed paste, chilli flakes and green chilli and sauté for another minute.
- Remove from the heat and sprinkle the roasted sesame seeds. Serve immediately.

Luchi

Ingredients

Refined flour (*maida*)	500 g
Salt	½ tsp
Melted ghee	3 tbsp
Vegetable oil for deep-frying	1 cup

Method

- Combine the flour, salt and sugar in a large bowl. Rub the melted ghee into it and add enough water to make a stiff but pliable dough.
- Cover the dough and leave to rest for 10 minutes.
- Make marble-sized balls of the dough and roll out into 2-inch discs (*luchi*).
- Heat the oil in a *kadai*.
- Slide each *luchi* along the side of the *kadai* into the hot oil. Gently splash the hot oil over the *luchi* till it puffs up. Flip it over and cook the other side. When pale pink in colour, remove with a slotted spoon and drain on absorbent paper.

To serve: Transfer the prawns to a serving dish or platter and serve with hot *luchi* and fresh green chillies.

My mother loved *chingri maach*, as prawns are known in Bengali. This was one of her favourite recipes.

Crunchy peppers which are a perfect complement to spongy mushrooms, doused in a creamy sauce – a treat for the taste buds! And what's even better – ready in a jiffy!

STIR-FRIED VEGETABLES IN ROSEMARY CREAM SAUCE

Pankaj Bhadouria

Preparation Time: 10 minutes
Cooking Time: 10 minutes
Serves: 3-4

Ingredients

Butter	3 tbsp
Red capsicum, cubed	1 medium
Yellow capsicum, cubed	1 medium
Green zucchini, cubed	1 medium
Fresh button mushrooms, cubed	200 g
Salt	½ tsp
Black pepper powder	½ tsp
Sauce	
Vegetable oil	1 tbsp
Onion, finely chopped	1 medium
Garlic, finely chopped	8 cloves
Fresh rosemary	2 sprigs
Low-fat fresh or packaged cream	1 cup
Salt	1 tsp
Black pepper powder	1 tsp

To serve

Garlic bread or crusty bread rolls

Method

- In a pan, heat the butter; add the vegetables and sauté lightly. Season with salt and pepper.

- For the sauce, heat the oil in a separate pan. Add the onion and sauté till translucent. Add the garlic and sauté for another minute.

- Add the rosemary and cream and bring to a slow boil. Season the sauce with salt and pepper. Remove from the heat.

To serve: Spoon the vegetables into the centre of a plate. Pour the sauce over the vegetables. Serve with garlic bread or crusty bread rolls.

BURNT GARLIC-CHILLI POT RICE

Pankaj Bhadouria

Preparation Time: 10 minutes
Cooking Time: 20 minutes
Serves: 4

Ingredients

Short grain rice	2 cups
Vegetable stock	1 litre
Vegetable oil	2 tbsp
Garlic, finely chopped	10 cloves
Fresh button mushrooms, quartered	200 g
Carrots, cut into round slices	2
Red capsicums, cut into thin strips	2
Green capsicums, cut into thin strips	2
Spring onions, sliced lengthways	6
Broccoli, separated into florets	100 g
Baby corn, sliced	50 g
Soy sauce	2 tbsp
Vinegar	2 tbsp
Salt	1 tsp
Black pepper powder	1 tsp
Dried chilli flakes	1 tsp
Chinese five spice powder*	½ tsp

To garnish

Chopped garlic, deep-fried golden brown	2 tbsp

* Chinese Five Spice Powder is a mixture of equal quantities of ground Szechwan pepper, star anise (*chakri phool*) cinnamon (*dalchini*), cloves (*laung*) and fennel seeds (*badi saunf*).

Method

- Cook the rice till almost done in 4 cups of vegetable stock. Transfer the rice to a large thick-bottomed pan.

- Heat the oil in another pan; add the garlic and sauté till brown. Add the vegetables and sauté for a few minutes.

- Add the soy sauce, vinegar, salt, pepper, chilli flakes and five spice powder and mix well.

- Place the vegetables on top of the rice. Pour the remaining stock over the vegetables and rice.

- Seal the pan with a tight-fitting lid and place in a hot oven for a few minutes. Alternatively, place the pan on a *tawa* over a high heat. Cook for a few minutes till the rice is cooked.

To serve: Place the rice and vegetables in bowls and sprinkle with the fried garlic just before serving.

A quick Chinese stir-fry with a burnt garlic pot rice can be your answer to a truly nail-biting match!

This is one of those never-fail recipes which is a hit with Mr. Husband, who loves tomato-based sauces and curries.

TANGY TOMATO CHICKEN

Pankaj Bhadouria

Preparation Time: 20 minutes
Cooking Time: 20 minutes
Serves: 4

Ingredients

Skinless, boneless chicken breasts	4 x150 g
Red chilli flakes	1 tsp
Dried oregano	½ tsp
Crushed black pepper	1 tsp
Salt	½ tsp
Olive oil	4 tbsp
Tangy Sauce	
Butter	2 tbsp
Garlic paste	1 tsp
Tomato purée	1 cup
Chicken stock	½ cup
Olive oil	2 tbsp
Salt	¼ tsp
Crushed black peppercorns	½ tsp
Garnish	
Finely chopped coriander	2 tsp
Freshly ground black pepper	

Method

- Wash the chicken breasts and pat dry. On one side, make deep slits half an inch apart to make pockets.

- Mix together the chilli flakes, oregano, crushed pepper, salt and oil.

- Rub some of the mixture on the chicken breasts. Fill the remaining mixture into the slits.

- Heat the olive oil in a frying pan and sear the chicken for 3 minutes on each side, or till tender. Remove from heat and keep covered.

- For the tangy sauce, heat the butter in a pan. Add the garlic paste and cook for a minute.

- Add the rest of the ingredients and bring to a boil, stirring continuously. Cook on a low heat for five minutes.

To serve: Arrange the chicken breasts on a platter and pour the sauce over the chicken. Sprinkle with chopped coriander and crushed pepper.

VEGETABLE SHASHLIK

Pankaj Bhadouria

Preparation Time: 10 minutes
Cooking Time: 20 minutes
Serves: 4

Ingredients

Large fresh button mushrooms	200 g
Yellow capsicum	1 medium
Red capsicum	1 medium
Green zucchini	1 medium
Marinade	
Oil	3 tbsp
Onions, finely sliced	2 large
Cloves	3
Nutmeg	¼ seed
Cinnamon	1-inch stick
Coriander seeds	1 tsp
Cumin seeds	1 tsp
Dried red chillies	2
Black peppercorns	1 tbsp
Garlic, finely chopped	8 cloves
Ginger, finely chopped	2 inches
Yoghurt	2 tbsp
Salt to taste	
To serve	
Onion rings	
Lemon wedges	

Method

- Wipe the mushrooms clean with a damp cloth and remove the stalks. Cut the capsicum into 1-inch squares. Cut the zucchini into chunks or rounds.

- For the marinade, heat the oil and fry the onions in batches to a deep golden brown. Remove and set aside to drain.

- In the same oil, sauté the whole spices for 30 seconds and remove. Reserve the oil to baste the vegetables.

- Grind the fried onions, fried spices, garlic, ginger, yoghurt and salt to a fine paste.

- Marinate all the prepared vegetables in the paste for 10 minutes.

- Thread the vegetables onto skewers and grill at 200°C/400°F/Gas 6 for about 10 minutes, basting with the reserved oil once or twice on all sides. Alternatively, cook the shashlik on a hot *tawa* or grill pan till done.

To serve: Arrange the shashliks on a platter and serve with onion rings and lemon wedges.

Unlike traditional shashliks, this one has fried onion paste in the marinade, giving it a unique colour and flavour.

No one can eat just one of these irresistible *pakode*!

AJWAINI MURGH PAKODE

Carom Seed-flavoured Chicken Bites

Chef Ajay Chopra

Preparation Time: 30 minutes
Cooking Time: 15 minutes
Serves: 4

Murgh Pakode

Ingredients

Boneless chicken leg meat	250 g
Ginger-garlic paste	5 tsp
Lemon juice	4 tsp
Salt	1 tsp
Oil for deep-frying	1 cup
Batter	
Bengal gram flour (*besan*)	300 g
Crushed roasted carom seeds (*ajwain*)	4 tsp
Red chilli powder	2 tsp
Coriander powder	1 tsp
Roasted cumin powder	1 tsp
Salt	1 tsp
Mustard oil	2 tsp

To serve

Green Chutney (recipe below)

Method

- Wash the chicken and pat dry. Cut into 1-inch pieces.
- Mix together the ginger-garlic paste, lemon juice and salt. Rub the mixture into the chicken, and leave to marinate for 20 minutes.
- For the batter, mix together all the ingredients, except the mustard oil, till smooth.
- Heat the mustard oil; add to the batter and stir vigorously to mix.
- Heat the oil in a *kadai*.
- Dip the marinated chicken pieces into the batter and deep-fry till golden brown. Remove with a slotted spoon and drain on absorbent paper.

Green Chutney

Ingredients

Green coriander	1 cup
Mint leaves	1 cup
Ginger, chopped	1 inch
Garlic, chopped	3-4 cloves
Green chillies, chopped	2
Lemon juice	4 tsp
Salt	½ tsp
Dried mango powder (*amchur*)	1 tsp

Method

- Grind or process all the ingredients in a blender to a fine paste. Adjust seasoning.

To serve: Arrange the *pakode* in a dish and serve with a bowl of green chutney on the side.

AKHROTI SUBZ SHIKAMPURI KEBAB

Vegetable Kebabs with Walnuts

Chef Ajay Chopra

Preparation Time: 35 minutes
Cooking Time: 15 minutes
Serves: 2

Ingredients

Carrot, diced	1 large
French beans, diced	100 g
Blanched green peas	100 g
Cauliflower florets	50 g
Potatoes, boiled and peeled	200 g
Green chillies, finely chopped	2
Ginger, grated	2 inches
Roasted gram (*daria dal*) powder	3½ tbsp
Roasted cumin powder	2 tsp
Cardamom powder	½ tsp
Chaat masala	1 tsp
Salt	2 tsp
Roasted, chopped walnuts	4 tbsp
Oil, for deep-frying	½ cup

To serve

Green Chutney (page 33)

Method

- Blanch all the vegetables, except the potatoes, and process them together coarsely in a blender. Place in a piece of muslin and squeeze gently to remove excess water.

- Mash the boiled potatoes and mix together with the processed vegetables.

- Add the green chillies, ginger, roasted gram powder, roasted cumin powder, cardamom powder, *chaat masala* and salt.

- Reserve a few small pieces of walnut, and add the rest to the vegetable mixture and mix well. Adjust seasoning.

- Shape the mixture into small patties and press a small piece of reserved walnut into each one.

- Heat the oil in a *kadai* and deep-fry the patties till golden brown. Remove and drain on absorbent paper.

To serve: Arrange the kebabs on a platter and serve with green chutney on the side.

These melt-in-the-mouth kebabs are a
delicious vegetarian version of the iconic
Hyderabadi mutton kebabs.

This is one of those dishes that is ready in a flash.
Just turn up the heat under a wok or pan and you
are good to go!

MUSHROOM AND SPINACH STIR-FRY

Chef Ajay Chopra

Preparation Time: 20 minutes
Cooking Time: 15 minutes
Serves: 4

Ingredients

Vegetable oil	4 tbsp
Cumin seeds	2 tbsp
Onions, sliced	2 large
Fresh button mushrooms	325 g
Cumin powder	½ tsp
Red chilli powder	1 tsp
Salt	½ tsp
Tomatoes, sliced	3 large
Spinach, chopped	400 g
Garam masala	¼ tsp
Dried fenugreek leaves (*kasoori methi*), powdered	½ tsp

To serve

Green salad

Method

- Heat the oil in a pan or wok over medium heat and add the cumin seeds. When they start to change colour, add the onions and sauté until golden brown.

- Add the mushrooms and sauté until they begin to soften.

- Add the cumin powder, chilli powder and salt and cook, stirring, for a couple of minutes.

- Add the sliced tomatoes and cook for 5-6 minutes. Add the spinach and cook, stirring continuously, until wilted.

- Sprinkle in the *garam masala* and dried fenugreek leaves, and adjust the seasoning.

To serve: Transfer the stir-fried mushrooms and spinach to a bowl and serve with a green salad.

SPINACH AND MOZZARELLA SAMOSAS

Chef Kunal Kapoor

Preparation Time: 30 minutes
Cooking Time: 30 minutes
Serves: 12 Samosas

Ingredients

Refined flour (*maida*)	500 g
Salt	1 tsp
Ghee	75 g
Water	¾ cup
Vegetable oil for deep-frying	
Filling	
Butter	1½ tbsp
Finely chopped garlic	2 tbsp
Onions, finely chopped	2 large
Green chilli, finely chopped	1
Finely chopped spinach, washed	4 cups
Salt to taste	
Turmeric powder	1 tsp
Red chilli powder	2 tsp
Coriander powder	2 tsp
Black pepper powder	1 tsp
Mozzarella cheese, grated	100 g
To serve	
Tomato sauce	

Method

- Rub the flour, salt and ghee together with your fingertips, till the mixture resembles coarse breadcrumbs.

- Mix in the water and knead to make a stiff dough. Set aside, covered, for 15 minutes.

- For the filling, heat the butter in a pan and add the garlic, onion and green chilli together. Sauté lightly for a few minutes.

- Add the chopped spinach, salt to taste and the rest of the spices. Sauté till the spinach wilts.

- Remove from the heat and spread out on a clean platter to cool.

- When cold, add the grated mozzarella and mix well.

- Divide the dough into 12 small balls and roll them out into thin circles. Place some mixture in the centre, moisten the edges of the dough and fold over to make half-moon shapes. Press the edges with the back of a fork to seal tightly.

- Heat the oil in a *kadai* and deep-fry the *samosas* till golden brown and crisp. Drain on absorbent paper.

To serve: Arrange the hot *samosas* on a platter and serve with tomato sauce.

Spinach and mozzarella are a marriage made in heaven. Enclosed in crisp pastry, they transport one to even greater celestial heights.

These rich, flaky *paranthe*, a legacy of the royal *dastarkhwans* of Awadh, are delicious eaten on their own, or with just a dollop of plain yoghurt or pickle.

WARQI PARANTHE

Crisp layered flatbreads

Chef Kunal Kapoor

Preparation Time: 30 minutes
Cooking Time: 10 minutes
Serves: 4

Ingredients

Milk	¾ cup
Green cardamom powder	1 tsp
Screw pine (*kewra*) water	1 tsp
Rose water	1 tsp
Sugar	1 tbsp
Salt	1 tsp
Semolina (*sooji*)	3 tbsp
Refined flour (*maida*)	400 g
Desi ghee	150 g

Method

- Pour the milk into a bowl and add the cardamom powder, *kewra* water, rose water, sugar, salt and semolina. Mix well and set aside for 5 minutes.

- Place the flour in a wide flat metal tray and make a well in the centre. Pour in the milk mixture and knead to make a soft dough.

- Spread the dough out and add three-fourths of the ghee to it a little by little, kneading well till all the ghee is absorbed by the dough. Rest the dough for 5 minutes and then divide into 8 equal balls.

- Roll out each ball of dough and spread half teaspoon ghee on it. Cut the dough with a knife from the centre towards the circumference. Start at one cut end and roll to make a cone. Leave to rest for 10 minutes. Flatten the dough and roll out into a thin round *parantha*.

- Heat a *tawa* and add a little ghee. Place a *parantha* on it and cook for a few seconds. Drizzle liberally with ghee and turn the *parantha* over. Press down with a clean piece of cloth to ensure it cooks and browns evenly. Turn over again and cook the other side. Remove from the heat.

To serve: Arrange the *paranthe* on a platter or in a basket and serve hot with *korma* or kebabs

PANCH PHORAN PRAWNS

Prawns coated with Bengali spices and fried

Chef Kunal Kapoor

Preparation Time: 15 minutes
Cooking Time: 15 minutes
Serves: 4

Ingredients

Prawns	450 g
Salt	1 tsp
Juice of 1 lemon	
Ginger paste	2 tsp
Garlic paste	2 tsp
Mustard sauce (*kasundi*)	2 tbsp
Panch phoran*, coarsely crushed	2 tbsp
Vegetable oil	2 tbsp

To serve

Thinly sliced lemon

Extra mustard sauce (*kasundi*)

*Panch phoran is a Bengali spice mix of equal quantities of onion seeds (*kalonji*), cumin seeds (*jeera*), fenugreek seeds (*methi dana*), fennel (*badi saunf*) and mustard seeds (*rai*).

Method

- Wash, peel and devein the prawns.
- Mix together the salt, lemon juice, ginger and garlic pastes and *kasundi*. Rub the paste into the prawns and leave to marinate for half an hour.
- Coat the marinated prawns with the crushed *panch phoran*.
- Heat the oil on a *tawa* and cook the prawns on both sides till tender and crisp on the outside.

To serve: Arrange the prawns in a dish, garnish with sliced lemon and serve with extra *kasundi* on the side.

Kasundi, the pungent Bengali mustard sauce, is what gives the prawns an unforgettable flavour unique to Bengali cuisine.

Gourmet

Awadhi *biryanis* are very different from their Hyderabadi cousins.
Here, the interplay of subtle flavours and aromas allows one to
savour the whole dish without any one ingredient dominating the
others. The hot *biryani* accompanied by a cool garlic-flavoured
burani is pure pleasure on a plate.

AWADHI SUBZ BIRYANI AUR BURANI

Aromatic Rice Layered with Vegetables and Served with
Garlic-Flavoured Yoghurt

Pankaj Bhadouria

Preparation Time: 40 minutes
Cooking Time: 40 minutes
Serves: 6

Biryani

Ingredients

Basmati rice	400 g
Ghee	7 tbsp
Onions, sliced	2 large
Black cumin seeds (*shahi jeera*)	1 tsp
Cloves	8
Cinnamon	2 x 1-inch sticks
Mace (*javitri*)	1 whole piece
Grated nutmeg	¼ tsp
Black peppercorns	1 tsp
Ginger paste	3 tbsp
Garlic paste	3 tbsp
Shelled green peas	100 g
Baby potatoes	100 g
Small cauliflower florets	100 g
French beans, cut into 1-inch pieces	100 g
Carrots, sliced diagonally	100 g
Salt to taste	
Black pepper powder	1 tsp
Yoghurt	½ cup
Black cardamoms	4
Green cardamoms	4
Bay leaves (*tej patta*)	2
Fresh mint leaves, finely chopped	½ cup
A few drops of rose water	
A few drops of screw pine (*kewra*) water	
Unsalted butter	2 tbsp
Wheat flour dough, to seal the dish	

Method

- Wash the rice and soak in water for half an hour.

- Heat 4 tablespoons of ghee in a pan; fry the sliced onion in batches to a golden brown and remove with a slotted spoon. Drain on absorbent paper.

- In the same pan, sauté half the black cumin seeds till they begin to sizzle. Add 2 cloves, 1 cinnamon stick, half the mace, the nutmeg and peppercorns and sauté till fragrant.

- Add the ginger and garlic pastes and sauté for 1 minute. Add the vegetables and sauté over a low heat for 1-2 minutes. Add salt, pepper and the yoghurt and cook till the vegetables are almost tender.

- In the meanwhile, in a separate large pan, bring 8 cups water to a boil with 2 teaspoons of salt.

- Tie the remaining cloves, cinnamon stick, mace and black cumin seeds, the black cardamoms and 2 green cardamoms in a piece of muslin to make a small bundle (*potli*), and add to the water with the bay leaves.

- Cook on a low heat for 15-20 minutes to allow the spices to infuse the water with their flavour.

- Drain the rice and add to the pan and cook till half done. Remove from the heat and strain. Reserve the strained water. Stir the remaining ghee into the rice and set aside.

- To assemble the *biryani*, spread half the fried onions at the base of a deep heavy-bottomed heatproof casserole. Spread half the rice over the onions.

Spread a layer of the vegetables and the chopped mint over the rice. Cover with the remaining rice and top with the remaining fried onion. Sprinkle the rose water and *kewra* water over the rice.

- Dot the rice with the unsalted butter. Pour in 1 cup of the strained water. Cover the casserole and seal it with the dough. Place on a hot *tawa* and cook on a low heat till steam begins to escape. Remove from the heat and leave to stand for 2 minutes. Break the dough seal, uncover the casserole and fluff up the rice with a fork.

Burani

Ingredients

Yoghurt	250 g
Garlic, crushed	4-5 cloves
Salt	½ tsp
Chilli flakes	½ tsp

Method

- Strain or whisk the yoghurt till smooth. Transfer to a bowl and mix in the rest of the ingredients. Place in a refrigerator to chill.

To serve: Transfer the *biryani* to a platter and serve with the *burani* on the side.

FISH IN COCONUT CURRY

Pankaj Bhadouria

Preparation Time: 15 minutes
Cooking Time: 15-20 minutes
Serves: 4

Ingredients

Firm white fish fillets	4 (300 g)
Coconut oil	2 tsp
Mustard seeds	1 tsp
Fresh curry leaves	10
Split black lentils (*urad dal*)	1 tsp
Split Bengal gram (*chana dal*)	1 tsp
Dried red chillies	3-4
Turmeric powder	1 tsp
Finely sliced onions	½ cup
Thin tomato strips	½ cup
Fresh or packaged coconut milk	1½ cups
Lemon juice	1 tsp
Salt	½ tsp

To serve

Steamed rice

Banana leaves

Method

- Wash and clean the fish fillets. Pat dry and cut into 2-inch pieces.

- Heat the oil in a deep pan and fry the mustard seeds till they begin to splutter. Add the curry leaves and both *dals* and fry till golden brown.

- Add the whole red chillies, turmeric powder and onions and sauté till the onions turn pink.

- Add the tomatoes and coconut milk and bring to a boil, stirring continuously.

- Add the fish and cook on a low heat till the fish is tender and the curry thickens slightly.

- Gently stir in the lemon juice and salt and remove from the heat.

To serve: Place a portion of rice on a banana leaf-lined plate, and top with the fish and curry.

This is my version of a South Indian curry that I have always enjoyed. Team it up with simple steamed rice and some crisp poppadums for a soul-satisfying meal. The curry dish tastes equally good prepared with freshwater or saltwater fish.

All the exotic and aromatic flavours
of the Middle East on a platter.

CHICKPEA KEBABS WITH COUSCOUS, TAHINA AND ARABIC SALAD

Pankaj Bhadouria

Preparation Time: 40 minutes plus soaking
Cooking Time: 20 minutes
Serves: 4

Chickpea Kebabs

Ingredients

Chickpeas (*Kabuli chana*)	250 g
Tabasco sauce	1 tsp
Very finely chopped garlic	1 tbsp
Very finely chopped ginger	1 tbsp
Finely chopped coriander	1 tsp
Dried oregano	1 tsp

Method

- Soak the chickpeas in water to cover for at least 6 hours. Drain and cook in fresh water till tender. Drain and spread out on a kitchen towel to dry.

- Process or grind the chickpeas to a coarse paste. Transfer to a bowl and add the remaining ingredients, except the oil, and mix well. Divide the mixture into 10 portions and shape into flat oblong kebabs.

Freshly ground pepper	1 tsp
Salt	½ tsp
Olive oil, for shallow-frying	½ cup

- Shallow-fry in moderately hot oil till light golden brown on all sides. Drain on absorbent paper.

Vegetable Couscous

Ingredients

Couscous or broken wheat (*dalia*)	250 g
Yellow capsicum, finely diced	1 medium
Red capsicum, finely diced	1 medium
Green capsicum, finely diced	1 medium
Fresh corn kernels	4 tbsp
Salt	1 tsp
Freshly ground black pepper	1 tsp
Vegetable stock	1 cup
Finely chopped parsley	2 tbsp

Method

- Place the couscous in a bowl. Add the capsicums, corn, salt and pepper, and mix well.
- Heat the stock and pour over the couscous mixture. Cover and leave to stand for five minutes till the stock has been absorbed and the couscous grains are light and fluffy.
- Garnish with the finely chopped parsley.

Tahina

Ingredients

Sesame seeds	½ cup
Garlic, chopped	3 cloves
Salt	½ tsp
Olive oil	1 tbsp
Lemon juice	½ cup
Finely chopped fresh parsley	1 tsp

Method

- Dry-roast the sesame seeds. Soak in 1 cup of warm water for 20 minutes and process or grind to a smooth paste.
- Add the garlic, salt, olive oil and lemon juice, and process till smooth.
- Transfer to a bowl and garnish with the chopped parsley.

Arabic Salad

Ingredients

Cucumbers, peeled	2 medium
Red tomatoes, quartered	2 large
Baby spinach leaves	12
Finely chopped coriander leaves	3 tbsp
Lemon juice	1 tbsp
Olive oil	2 tbsp

Method

- Toss all the ingredients together and transfer to a serving bowl.

To serve: Arrange the kebabs on a platter with the couscous. Serve with the tahina and Arabic salad.

FENUGREEK-FLAVOURED FISH WITH LEMON BUTTER SAUCE

Pankaj Bhadouria

Preparation Time: 20 minutes
Cooking Time: 15 minutes
Serves: 4

Ingredients

For the fish

Firm white fish fillets	4 (300 g)
Salt	½ tsp
Lemon juice	4 tsp
Coriander seeds	1 tsp
Black peppercorns	1 tsp
Cumin seeds	½ tsp
Dried fenugreek leaves (*kasoori methi*)	1½ tbsp
Caraway seeds (*shia jeera/vilayati jeera*)	½ tsp
Red chilli flakes	1 tsp
Vegetable oil	1 tbsp

For the lemon butter sauce

Onion, finely chopped	1 large
Garlic, finely chopped	4-5 cloves
Frozen butter	50 g
Lemon juice	2½ tbsp
Salt	¼ tsp
Black pepper powder	½ tsp

Method

For the fish

- Wash and clean the fish fillets and pat them dry. Sprinkle with the salt and lemon juice and marinate for 12-15 minutes.

- Dry-roast the coriander seeds, peppercorns and cumin seeds in a pan and grind coarsely. Dry-roast the dried fenugreek leaves and crush between your palms. Mix together the fenugreek leaves, ground spices, caraway seeds and chilli flakes. Transfer to a plate.

- Roll the fish fillets in the mixture to coat evenly on all sides.

- Heat the oil in a frying pan and sear the fish on each side for 1 minute, and fry till opaque and flaky in the centre.

For the sauce

- Heat half the butter in a small pan till it browns slightly. Add the finely chopped onions and sauté till translucent.

- Add the garlic and sauté over low heat for a minute. Add the lemon juice and season with salt and pepper.

- Remove from the heat and add the rest of the frozen butter, whisking vigorously till thick.

To serve: Arrange the fish fillets on a platter and serve the lemon butter on the side.

Traditional Punjabi *kadai masala*, with *kasoori methi*, which I love, was the inspiration for this dish. Add *ajwain*, without which fish is rarely cooked in Punjab, and the blandest fish will become irresistible.

Traditional Awadhi recipes are closely-guarded secrets. I have tried to recreate the magic of the melt-in-your-mouth kebabs, which are so soft that they are difficult to serve as cocktail snacks. I decided once to put them into tart cases to make them easier to handle and they have been a hit ever since! You can substitute the tart cases with good old *mathri*, which work just as well!

GILAOUTI KEBAB TARTS

Melt-in-the-mouth Mutton Patties on a Bed of Onion
Salad in Crisp Tart Shells

Pankaj Bhadouria

Preparation Time: 25 minutes plus marination
Cooking Time: 20 minutes
Serves: 4-5

Ingredients

Gilaouti kebabs

Minced mutton	250 g
Unripe green papaya paste	2 tbsp
Ginger paste	1 tsp
Garlic paste	1 tsp
Salt to taste	
Cumin seeds	1½ tsp
Aniseed (*saunf*)	2½ tbsp
Coriander seeds	1½ tbsp
Poppy seeds (*khus khus*)	1 tsp
Ghee	½ tbsp

Method

For the gilaouti kebabs

- Marinate the minced mutton in a mixture of unripe papaya paste, ginger and garlic pastes and salt to taste for at least 3-4 hours.

- Dry-roast the cumin seeds, aniseed, coriander seeds and poppy seeds separately in a pan or on a *tawa*.

- In a small pan, heat the ghee to smoking point. Add the nutmeg, cinnamon and mace, stir and remove after 5 seconds.

- Heat the oil in a *kadai* and deep-fry the finely sliced onion till crisp and brown. Drain on absorbent paper.

Grated nutmeg (*jaiphal*)	¼ tsp
Cinnamon	1-inch stick
Vegetable oil for deep-frying	
Mace (*javitri*)	1 whole piece
Onion, finely sliced	1 large
Black pepper powder	½ tsp
Red chilli powder	½ tsp
Garlic cloves	5-6
Roasted gram flour (*besan*)	2 tbsp
Cloves	3
Coal pieces	2-3
Tart shells	
Flour	250 g
Chilled butter	125 g
Cold water	5 tsp
Onion salad	
Onions, finely sliced	2 large
Fresh green coriander leaves	2 tbsp
Green chillies, finely chopped	3 small
Salt	½ tsp
Pepper	½ tsp
Lemon juice	1 tbsp
Mint chutney	
Chopped fresh mint	½ cup
Chopped coriander	½ cup
Lemon juice	1 tbsp
Green chillies, chopped	2
Salt	½ tsp

- Grind to a paste the roasted spices, pepper, chilli powder, fried onions, salt, garlic, gram flour and the spices cooked in the ghee. Mix well into the marinated mince.

- Heat a piece of coal over an open flame till red hot and smoking and place in a small bowl. Place the mince in a large bowl. Make a depression in the centre and place the bowl with the coal in it. Add the cloves to the coal and cover the bowl immediately. Leave to stand for 5 to 10 minutes. This is the traditional method of smoking food called 'dunghar'.

- Shape the smoked mince mixture into ten 2½-inch round patties.

- Heat a little oil in a frying pan and cook the patties on each side for 3 minutes or until golden brown. Remove and drain on absorbent paper.

For the tart shells

- Sift the flour thrice into a bowl to ensure air is incorporated into it. Rub in the cold butter with your fingertips till the mixture resembles fine breadcrumbs.

- Add 5 tablespoons of cold water to bind it together. Do not knead the dough. Wrap the dough in cling film and refrigerate it for 10-15 minutes.

- Preheat an oven to 200°C/400°F/Gas 6.

- Remove the dough from the refrigerator and roll out into a quarter-inch-thick rectangle on a floured surface.

- Cut out ten 4-inch rounds with a pastry cutter and press into tart moulds. Prick the pastry with a fork and place on a baking tray. Bake blind for 10 minutes in the preheated oven.

- Remove from the oven and turn out of the moulds. Place on a wire rack to cool.

For the onion salad

- Toss all the ingredients together in a bowl.

For the mint chutney

- Process all the ingredients together in a blender.

To serve: Place a little onion salad in each tart shell. Place a kebab on top and spoon a dollop of mint chutney on the kebab.

GINGER CHICKEN IN SPICED HONEY SAUCE WITH PARSLEY RICE

Pankaj Bhadouria

Preparation Time: 30 minutes
Cooking Time: 20 minutes
Serves: 4

Ginger Chicken

Ingredients

Chicken drumsticks	400 g
Ginger juice*	3 tbsp
Salt to taste	
Vegetable oil for deep-frying	
Onions, finely sliced	3
Cumin seeds, roasted	1 tsp
Coriander seeds, roasted	1 tsp
Shallots, peeled	8-10
Cinnamon	1-inch stick
Onion, finely chopped	1
Ginger paste	1 tbsp
Tomato purée	4 tbsp
Black pepper powder	½ tsp
Honey	3 tsp
Cardamom powder	2 tsp

* To make ginger juice, grind fresh ginger to a paste,
  squeeze out the juice and strain.

Method

- Wash, clean and remove the skin of the chicken legs. Marinate the chicken in the ginger juice and salt for 15 minutes.

- Heat the oil in a *kadai* and deep-fry the sliced onions till golden brown. Remove, cool and grind to a smooth paste.

- Grind the roasted cumin seeds and coriander seeds together to a fine powder.

- Heat 1 tablespoon oil in a frying pan and sauté the shallots. Remove and set aside to drain.

- In the same frying pan, heat 2 tablespoons oil; add the cinnamon stick and when it sizzles, add the chopped onion and ginger paste and sauté till the onion is translucent.

- Stir in the brown onion paste, ground cumin-coriander powder, tomato purée and pepper, and cook for 5-7 minutes. Add salt and half a cup of water and cook on a low heat for 2-3 minutes.

- Add the honey, fried shallots and cardamom powder, and cook for 1 more minute and remove from heat.

- Heat 1 tablespoon oil in a large frying pan and cook the marinated chicken on high heat till tender, basting with the marinating juices, and turning over to cook evenly on all sides.

Parsely Rice

Ingredients

Basmati rice	1 cup
Butter	3 tbsp
Finely chopped fresh parsley	½ cup

Method

- Cook the rice in a pan with 2 cups of water till tender.

- Add the butter and chopped parsley and toss gently to mix.

To serve: Arrange the chicken in a serving bowl, pour the gravy on top and serve with parsley rice.

During the MasterChef grooming classes I came up with this dish, which won me a lot of praise. The fiery colour belies the delicate flavours of the dish.

Soaked apricots and almonds, which are used liberally in Mughlai cooking, have a soothing and cooling effect in summer. These delicately flavoured kebabs are a treat for the palate and easy on the stomach as well.

GOLI KEBAB AUR KHEERA PUDINA RAITA

Marble-shaped Chicken and Apricot Kebabs with a
Cucumber and Mint Yoghurt Dip

Pankaj Bhadouria

Preparation Time: 20 minutes
Cooking Time: 40 minutes
Serves: 6

Goli Kebabs

Ingredients

Dried apricots	15
Almonds	15
Minced chicken	750 g
Garlic, finely chopped	4 cloves
Ginger, finely chopped	1 inch
Split Bengal gram (*chana dal*)	100 g
Dried red chillies	5
Black peppercorns	6-8
Cloves	2
Cinnamon	2-inch stick
Salt	1 tsp
Egg, beaten	1 small
Poppy seeds (*khus khus*)	100 g
Oil	1 cup

Method

- Slit the apricots and carefully remove the pits. Soak the apricots and the almonds in warm water. Peel the almonds. Place an almond inside each apricot and set aside.

- Put the minced chicken, garlic, ginger, *chana dal*, red chillies, peppercorns, cloves and cinnamon in a heavy-bottomed pan with 2 cups water and the salt. Cover and cook till the *dal* is soft. Uncover the pan and cook till the water evaporates. Remove from heat and set aside to cool.

- Grind the chicken mixture to a fine, smooth paste in a blender. Mix in the beaten egg. Divide the mixture into 15 portions.

- Flatten each portion of mince on the moistened palm of your hand and place a stuffed apricot in the middle. Gather the edges together to enclose the apricot and roll into a ball. Roll the ball in poppy seeds to coat well all round.

- Heat the oil in a *kadai* and add the kebabs in batches. Reduce the heat and deep-fry till golden brown. Remove with a slotted spoon and drain on absorbent paper.

Kheera Pudina Raita

Ingredients

Yoghurt, whisked	1 cup
Cucumbers, finely diced	2 medium
Fresh mint leaves, finely sliced	20
Salt	½ tsp
Crushed black pepper	½ tsp

Method

- Whisk the yoghurt in a bowl. Add the rest of the ingredients and mix well. Place in a refrigerator to chill for a while before serving.

To serve: Arrange the kebabs on a platter and serve with the *raita* on the side.

MASALEDAAR RAAN AUR KESARI AKHROT RAITA

Roasted Spiced Leg of Lamb with Saffron-flavoured Yoghurt and Walnut Sauce

Pankaj Bhadouria

Preparation Time: 20 minutes plus marination
Cooking Time: 1 ½ hours
Serves: 6-8

Masaledaar Raan

Ingredients

1 leg of lamb (approx. 2 kg)	
Unripe green papaya paste	3 tbsp
Vegetable oil	½ cup
Spice Rub	
Star anise (*chakri phool*)	2 whole pieces
Dried Kashmiri chillies	6
Cumin seeds	1 tsp
Green cardamoms	6
Cinnamon	1-inch stick
Fennel seeds (*badi saunf*)	1 tsp
Dried ginger powder (*sonth*)	1 tsp
Black peppercorns	1 tbsp
Salt	½ tsp
To serve	
Sliced onions	
Pickled red and green chilli rings	

Method

- Clean and wash the leg of lamb. Slice the meat off the bone at the top and push it downwards. Wrap the exposed bone in foil so that it does not brown in the oven.

- Rub the papaya paste into the meat and set aside for an hour.

- For the spice rub, grind all the ingredients to make a coarse powder. Reserve some of the rub for garnishing, and mix the rest into the oil. Apply generously over the meat.

- Preheat an oven to 240°C/475°F/Gas 9. Grease a roasting tin.

- Place the lamb in the tin and cover with a sheet of aluminium foil.

- Place in the preheated oven and cook for 1 hour. Remove the foil, turn the leg of lamb over and cook till tender and golden brown. Baste the meat occasionally with the oil.

- Alternatively, cook the lamb in a hot *tandoor*.

- Remove from the oven and leave to stand for a few minutes. Cut into thin slices and sprinkle with some of the rub.

Kesari Akhrot Raita

Ingredients

Yoghurt	1 cup
A few saffron threads	
Walnuts, coarsely crushed	2 tbsp
Salt	1 tsp

Method

- Whisk the yoghurt in a bowl. Add the rest of the ingredients and mix well.

- Place in a refrigerator to chill.

To serve: Arrange the slices of lamb on a platter and sprinkle with the reserved spice rub. Serve with chilled saffron walnut *raita* and marinated red and green chillies.

Leg of lamb is cooked in all parts of the world in different ways. Try out this delicious version, redolent of dried ginger and aniseed, and accompanied by a creamy saffron walnut *raita* for a quintessential Kashmiri experience.

This Burmese speciality is a do-it-yourself kind of dish, which leaves you free to add garnishes to suit your taste buds.

VEGETABLE KHAU SUEY

Pankaj Bhadouria

Preparation Time: 30 minutes
Cooking Time: 30 minutes
Serves: 4-6

Ingredients

Vegetable oil	1 tbsp
Onions, finely chopped	2 small
Garlic, finely chopped	6 cloves
Ginger, finely chopped	1 inch
Yellow zucchini, cubed	1
Green zucchini, cubed	1
Fresh button mushrooms, quartered	100 g
Turmeric powder	1 tsp
Chilli powder	1 tsp
Coconut milk	1 cup
Vegetable stock	1 cup
Salt	½ tsp
Gram flour (*besan*)	2 tbsp

Noodles

Hakka noodles	500 g
Oil	2 tbsp
Salt	1 tsp

Garnishes

Deep-fried sliced onions	¼ cup
Chopped coriander	2 tbsp
Green chillies, chopped	8-10
Garlic, chopped and fried	10-12 cloves
Boiled egg, chopped	1 small
Raw noodles, fried	50 g
Peanuts	¼ cup
Soya sauce	¼ cup
Lemons, quartered	2

Method

- In a pan, heat the oil and sauté the onions lightly. Add the garlic and ginger and sauté for a minute. Add all the prepared vegetables and turmeric powder and sauté for a few minutes.

- Stir in the chilli powder, coconut milk, vegetable stock and salt.

- Add the gram flour, made with a little water into a paste, and mix well. Bring to a boil, reduce the heat and simmer for a few minutes till the vegetables are tender and the gravy thickens slightly.

- Boil the noodles in plenty of water with the oil and salt till *al dente* (cooked but still firm to the bite). Remove from the heat and drain.

To serve: Divide the noodles among four bowls or soup plates. Pour the vegetables with the gravy on top of the noodles. Sprinkle a little of each of the garnishes on top.

PALAK PANEER AUR MAKKAI KI MATTHRI

Grilled Cottage Cheese on a Bed of Spinach with
Crisp Corn Crackers

Pankaj Bhadouria

Preparation Time: 20 minutes
Cooking Time: 20 minutes
Serves: 4

Palak Paneer

Ingredients

Cottage cheese (*paneer*)	250 g
Dried fenugreek leaves (*kasoori methi*), crushed	1 tsp
Vegetable oil	2 tbsp
Butter	1½ tbsp
Onion, finely chopped	1 medium
Garlic paste	1 tsp
Ginger paste	1 tsp
Salt	1 tsp
Black peppercorns, crushed	1 tsp
Red chilli powder	1 tsp
Coriander powder	½ tsp
Garam masala powder	½ tsp
Fresh spinach leaves, roughly chopped	500 g
Fresh cream	1 cup

Method

- Cut the *paneer* into 2-inch slices. Toss the *paneer* in the *kasoori methi*.

- Heat the oil in a grill pan and cook the *paneer* slices on both sides till golden brown. Set aside.

- Heat the butter in a pan; add the chopped onion, ginger and garlic pastes, and sauté till the onion turns pink.

- Add the salt, crushed pepper, chilli, coriander and *garam masala* powders and cook for a few minutes. Add the spinach and cook for a few minutes. Stir in the cream.

Makkai ki Matthri

Ingredients

Maize flour (*makkai ka atta*)	300 g
Refined flour (*maida*)	200 g
Warm water	300 ml
Salt	1 tsp
Vegetable oil	1 cup

Method

- Combine the maize flour and flour and knead with water to make a soft dough. Divide the dough into small marble-sized balls.

- Roll out each ball of dough into a 3-inch disc on a floured surface. Prick the discs with a fork to prevent them from puffing up.

- Heat the oil in a *kadai* and deep-fry the discs till crisp and golden. Drain on absorbent paper.

To serve: Ladle the spinach onto a platter, arrange the *paneer* fingers on top and serve with the corn crackers on the side.

Here is the ubiquitous *palak paneer* in a new avatar.
The crisp corn crackers provide a delightful contrast
to the firm *paneer* and chunky spinach sauce.

Paneer makhani is one of those dishes that can be found in any Indian restaurant anywhere in the world. The dish is traditionally cooked over a low heat for a very long time to allow the rich tomato flavour to infuse the *paneer*.

PANEER MAKHANI AUR KALONJI NAAN

Cottage Cheese in a Creamy Tomato Sauce Served
with Onion Seed Flatbread

Pankaj Bhadouria

Preparation Time: 30 minutes
Cooking Time: 30 minutes
Serves: 4

Paneer Makhani

Ingredients

Tomatoes, chopped	4 large
Onion, chopped	1 large
Ginger, chopped	2 inches
Garlic cloves, chopped	3
Butter	4 tbsp
Black cumin seeds (*shahi jeera*)	½ tsp
Tomato purée	3 tbsp
Cottage cheese (*paneer*), cut into 1-inch cubes	300 g
Black pepper powder	1 tsp
Red chilli powder	1 tsp
Salt	½ tsp
Dried fenugreek leaves (*kasoori methi*)	2 tbsp
Fresh cream	1 cup
Thin ginger strips	2 tbsp

To serve

Onion rings

Method

- Put the tomatoes, onion, ginger, garlic and 3 cups water into a pan and bring to a boil. Lower the heat and simmer for at least 15-20 minutes. Remove from the heat and cool. Purée the cooled mixture in a blender.

- In a pan, heat the butter; add the *shahi jeera* and sauté for 30 seconds. Stir in the puréed mixture and the tomato purée, and cook on a low heat for 10-15 minutes.

- Add the *paneer* to the simmering sauce. Gently stir in the pepper, chilli powder and salt.

- Dry-roast the dried fenugreek leaves in a pan. Set aside some for garnishing, crush the rest between your palms and add to the *paneer*. Cook for another 5 minutes for the *paneer* to absorb the flavour of the fenugreek.

- Finally, gently stir in the cream. Sprinkle with the ginger strips and reserved dried fenugreek leaves.

Kalonji Naan

Ingredients

Flour	500 g
Yoghurt	4 tbsp
Baking powder	2 tsp
Salt	½ tsp
Granulated sugar	½ tsp
Vegetable oil	2 tbsp
Onion seeds (*kalonji*)	1 tsp
Butter, for brushing	

Method

- Sift the flour into a bowl.

- Mix together the yoghurt, baking powder, salt, sugar and about 1 cup water. Add to the flour and knead to a smooth dough, adding more water as required. Set aside, covered, for 20 minutes.

- Add the oil and knead till all the oil is absorbed into the dough. Divide the dough into 8-10 balls.

- On a floured surface, roll out each ball into an oblong *naan*. Sprinkle some onion seeds on top and place in a hot *tandoor*. Cook till puffed up. Alternatively, grill on the top rack of an oven. Brush with butter and serve.

To serve: Ladle the *paneer* into a serving bowl, garnish with onion rings and serve with *kalonji naan* on the side.

NAVRATAN KORMA AUR DOSTI ROTI

Nine 'Jewels' in a Creamy Gravy Served
with Paper Thin Flatbreads

Pankaj Bhadouria

Preparation Time: 25 minutes
Cooking Time: 25 minutes
Serves: 4

Navratan Korma

Ingredients

Vegetable oil	1 cup
Fox nuts (*makhana*)	1 cup
Cashew nuts	50 g
Raisins (*kishmish*)	1 tbsp
French beans, cut into 1-inch pieces	4-5
Carrot, cut into ½-inch cubes	1 medium
Potato, cut into ½-inch cubes	1 medium
Small cauliflower florets	¼ cup
Shelled green peas	¼ cup
Cottage cheese (*paneer*), cut into ½-inch cubes	50 g
Fresh button mushrooms, halved	4 large

Korma Gravy

Pure ghee or vegetable oil	3 tbsp
Cloves	2
Cinnamon	1-inch stick
Green cardamoms	2
Boiled onion paste*	½ cup
Ginger paste	½ tbsp
Garlic paste	½ tbsp
White pepper powder	1 tsp
Yoghurt	2 tbsp
Green chillies, slit	2
Thick cream	3 tbsp
Salt	1 tsp

*For the boiled onion paste, roughly chop 2 medium onions and add ½ cup water. Bring to a boil and simmer, covered, for 10 minutes. Cool and grind to a paste.

Method

- Heat the oil and deep-fry the fox nuts and then half the cashew nuts. Drain on absorbent paper.

- Soak the remaining cashew nuts in warm water for 20 minutes. Drain and grind to a smooth paste along with the raisins.

- In a pan, bring 2 cups water with half a teaspoon salt to a boil. Add the beans, carrot, potato, cauliflower and peas and cook for 5-6 minutes, or till the vegetables are tender. Drain and refresh the vegetables in cold water.

- For the *korma* gravy, heat 3 tablespoons of ghee in a pan and add the cloves, cinnamon and split cardamoms and sauté for 30 seconds.

- Add the onion paste and sauté over a low heat for a few minutes. The onion paste should remain a translucent pink and not turn brown.

- Add the ginger and garlic pastes, white pepper powder and yoghurt, and stir well. Cook on a low heat for 2 minutes.

- Add the green chillies and cashew-raisin paste and continue to cook for 5 minutes. Add the cottage cheese, mushrooms and vegetables, half a teaspoon of salt and ¾ cup water. Bring to a boil, reduce the heat and simmer for 2 minutes.

- Add the fox nuts and cream and simmer for 2-3 minutes. Remove from heat.

Dosti Roti

Ingredients

Refined flour (*maida*)	1 cup
Wholewheat flour (*atta*)	1 cup
Salt	¼ tsp
Oil, plus for brushing the dough	2 tbsp

To serve: Transfer the *korma* to a bowl and serve the *roti* on the side.

Method

- Mix together the refined flour, wholewheat flour and salt and knead with a little water into a soft dough. Set the dough aside, covered, for 10 minutes.

- Add the oil to the dough and knead till all the oil is absorbed. Divide the dough into lemon-sized balls.

- Dust the balls with refined flour and roll out into 6-inch discs. Brush one disc liberally with oil. Place another disc over it. Dust well with flour and roll out the twin discs (*dosti*) into 12-inch circles.

- Heat a large *tawa*. Place a *dosti roti* on it and cook, pressing down lightly with a piece of cloth. Flip the *roti* and cook the other side as well, taking care not to cook it for too long or the *roti* will become crisp and hard.

- Remove from the *tawa* and immediately separate the two *roti*. Fold each one twice into a triangle and cover with a cloth immediately to keep it warm and soft.

Navratan means nine jewels and the dish has just that! The nine main ingredients shine in a creamy white *korma* gravy which is sweetened with raisins and cashew nuts.

The *dosti roti*, true to its name, is really two *rotis* cooked together. The *rotis* are paper thin, with one side a golden brown and the other a softer, paler shade. They are a good substitute for the more common *roomali roti*.

This is the dish - which I named 'Chicken Smiles'- that got me through the MasterChef Lucknow auditions. And it certainly put a smile on my face!

POPPY SEED-ENCRUSTED CHICKEN AND MINCED MUTTON ROULADES

Pankaj Bhadouria

Preparation Time: 20 minutes
Cooking Time: 20 minutes
Serves: 4-6

Ingredients

Boneless, skinless chicken breasts	3 x 150 g
Minced mutton	200 g
Chopped ginger	2 tsp
Chopped garlic	1 tsp
Green chilli sauce	1 tbsp
Salt	½ tsp
Black pepper powder	1 tsp
Egg	1
Poppy seeds (*khus khus*)	½ cup

To serve

Fresh green salad
Red chilli sauce

Method

- Split each chicken breast in half, slicing through without separating the halves. Open out like a sheet. Flatten with a meat hammer or rolling pin between 2 sheets of cling film to make a rectangle.

- In a bowl, mix together the minced mutton, chopped ginger and garlic, and green chilli sauce. Grind or process to a soft, smooth paste. Season with salt and pepper.

- Spread the ground mutton paste over the chicken breasts. Roll up tightly lengthways like Swiss rolls. Secure with toothpicks or wrap tightly in cling film. Refrigerate for an hour.

- Preheat an oven to 200°C/400°F/Gas 6.

- Whisk the egg with 1 tablespoon water to make an egg wash.

- Remove the toothpicks or cling film and brush the chicken rolls with the egg wash. Roll in the poppy seeds to coat evenly on all sides.

- Place the chicken rolls on a greased baking tray and bake in the preheated oven for 20 minutes till golden brown.

- Remove from the oven and cut the roulades into even slices.

To serve: Arrange the roulade slices on a platter, and serve with a fresh green salad and red chilli sauce.

POTATO GNOCCHI IN MARINARA SAUCE

Pankaj Bhadouria

Preparation Time: 30 minutes
Cooking Time: 35 minutes
Serves: 4

Ingredients

Marinara sauce

Tomatoes	1 kg
Tomato purée	300 g
Finely chopped parsley	2 tbsp
Chopped garlic	1 tsp
Dried oregano	¼ tsp
Salt	½ tsp
Black pepper powder	½ tsp
Olive oil	6 tbsp
Onion, finely chopped	1 medium
White wine	100 ml

Potato gnocchi

Potatoes	500 g
Salt	1½ tsp
Black pepper powder	1 tsp
Large egg	1
Refined flour (*maida*)	100 g
Grated nutmeg	¼ tsp
Butter	2 tbsp
Pitted black olives, sliced	100 g

To serve

Chopped fresh parsley	1 tbsp

Method

For the sauce

- Process the tomatoes, tomato purée, chopped parsley, garlic, oregano, salt and pepper in a blender till smooth.

- In a large pan, heat the olive oil and sauté the finely chopped onion for 2 minutes. Add the puréed tomato mixture and white wine. Cook on a low heat for 30 minutes, stirring occasionally. Keep warm.

For the gnocchi

- Put the potatoes into boiling water with 1 teaspoon salt and cook till done. Drain the potatoes and peel while still hot. Force the potatoes through a sieve with the back of a spoon.

- Add ½ teaspoon salt and the pepper, and then beat in the egg till it is completely incorporated. Add the flour, a little by little, and mix well to make a smooth dough. Add the nutmeg and knead the dough for a few minutes. If the dough gets sticky, add more flour. Divide the dough into 4 parts.

- Roll each part into a smooth long roll about 1 inch in diameter. Cut the roll into 1-inch long pieces.

- To shape the gnocchi, place a fork on a board. One by one, press and roll the gnocchi lightly over the tines of the fork to make ridges on one side. Make a depression with your thumb on the other side.

- Bring a large pan of water to a boil. Add 1 teaspoon salt and drop the gnocchi into the water in 2 batches.

- When the gnocchi rise to the surface, remove with a slotted spoon. Drain and toss immediately with the butter and sliced olives.

To serve: Place the gnocchi in individual plates and ladle some sauce over. Garnish with chopped parsley.

This is an Italian favourite which kids and adults enjoy alike. Simple, yet gratifying.

You must try out the barbecue sauce. I assure you it will turn out better than any bottled one available. Make sure that the mashed potato is creamy and smooth for a truly winning combination.

CROWN ROAST OF LAMB IN BARBECUE SAUCE WITH MASHED POTATO AND SAUTÉED VEGETABLES

Pankaj Bhadouria

Preparation Time: 30 minutes
Cooking Time: 1½ hours
Serves: 4

Roast Lamb

Ingredients

Rack of lamb	1 kg
Finely chopped fresh rosemary	2 tsp
Vegetable oil, for basting	3 tbsp

Method

- Clean and wash the lamb well. Cover the bones with foil. Twist the rack to form a crown. Tie it around the centre.

- For the barbecue sauce, heat the oil in a pan and sauté the garlic and chopped onions for a few minutes till soft.

Barbecue sauce

Vegetable oil	2 tbsp
Garlic, finely chopped	6 cloves
Finely chopped onion	2 tbsp
Tomato purée	1 cup
Mutton stock	1 cup
Sugar	1 tbsp
Vinegar	1 tbsp
Worcestershire sauce	3 tbsp
Salt	½ tsp
Black pepper powder	1 tsp
Dried rosemary	1 tsp

- Add the remaining ingredients, bring to a boil and cook on a low heat till the mixture thickens slightly. Cook for 5 minutes longer and remove from heat.
- Brush the lamb liberally with the barbecue sauce and marinate for 30 minutes.
- Preheat an oven to 200°C/400°F/Gas 6.
- Place the lamb in a greased roasting tin. Sprinkle with rosemary and cover the baking tin with foil.
- Cook the lamb in the preheated oven for 1 hour. Remove the foil and baste the meat with oil and sauce. Cook till the meat is tender and golden brown.
- Heat any leftover sauce in the roasting tin with a little stock and keep warm.

Creamy Mashed Potato

Ingredients

Large potatoes	3
Salt	1 tsp
Black pepper powder	1 tsp
Fresh cream	½ cup
Butter	4 tbsp

Method

- Place potatoes in a pan of cold water to cover and bring to a boil. Lower the heat and cook till the potatoes are tender. Peel and mash the potatoes well.
- Place the mashed potatoes in a pan with the rest of the ingredients and cook on a low heat till heated through. Whisk with a wire whisk or fork, or beat vigorously with a spoon till fluffy, adding more cream or butter if required.

Sautéed Vegetables

Ingredients

Green capsicum, cut into round slices	1
Yellow zucchini, cut into round slices	1
Cherry tomatoes	10
Olive oil	1 tbsp
Salt	½ tsp
Black pepper powder	½ tsp

Method

- In a frying pan, sauté all the vegetables in olive oil. Season with salt and pepper.

To serve: Place the rack of lamb on a platter and pour the sauce over. Arrange the mashed potato and sautéed vegetables on the side.

Or, slice the rack and place 2 lamb chops on individual plates and drizzle with the sauce. Serve with mashed potato and some sautéed vegetables.

STUFFED VEGETABLES WITH TAMARIND SAUCE

Pankaj Bhadouria

Preparation Time: 40 minutes
Cooking Time: 40 minutes
Serves: 4

Ingredients

Yellow capsicums	2 large
Red capsicums	2 large
Onions	2 large
Honey, for glazing	4 tbsp
Filling	
Garlic	10 cloves
Butter	4 tbsp
Bread	8 slices
Boiled red kidney beans (*rajma*)	1½ cups
Toasted pine nuts (*chilgoza*)	¼ cup
Salt	½ tsp
Black pepper powder	1 tsp
Grated processed cheddar cheese	¼ cup
Mixed dried herbs	1 tsp
Vegetable oil	4 tsp
Tomato purée	3 tbsp
Tamarind Sauce	
Tamarind	50 g
Warm water	1 cup
Sugar	2 tbsp
Salt	1 tsp
Black pepper powder	¼ tsp
Chilli powder	½ tsp
Cumin powder	½ tsp

Method

For the stuffed vegetables

- Cut off the tops of the capsicums and remove the insides.

- Peel the onions and leave them whole. Place the onions with the bay leaves in a pan of boiling water which covers the onions completely.

- Reduce the heat and simmer for 10-12 minutes. Drain and set aside to cool. Reserve half a cup water.

- Cut a small piece off the top and bottom of each onion so that it can stand upright. Using a sharp knife and a spoon, scoop out all but 3-4 outer layers of the onions. Chop the scooped out portions and set aside.

- For the filling, peel and crush the garlic and mix well with the butter. Spread the garlic butter on the slices of bread and toast in an oven till crisp. Cool and cut the bread into small squares or croûtons.

- Mix together the boiled beans, pine nuts, croûtons, salt, and grated cheese in a bowl. Add half the mixed herbs.

- Heat the oil in a pan; add the reserved chopped onions and sauté for 3-4 minutes. Add the tomato purée, remaining herbs and salt and cook for 2 minutes.

- Add the reserved water in which the onions were cooked and cook on a low heat for 8-10 minutes. Remove from heat, leave to cool for a few minutes and process in a blender.

- Transfer the mixture to a bowl. Add the bean mixture and mix well.

- Preheat the oven to 180°C/350°F/Gas 4.

- Fill the capsicum and onion shells with the bean mixture. Place the stuffed vegetables on a greased baking tray and bake in the preheated oven for 15 minutes.

- Brush with the honey and serve hot.

For the tamarind sauce

- Soak the tamarind for 30 minutes in the warm water. Mash the pulp and strain through a fine sieve or piece of muslin.

- Heat a pan; add the sugar and tamarind pulp along with the remaining ingredients.

- Cook the pulp till it thickens to the consistency of a sauce. Pour into a bowl or small jug.

To serve: Arrange the stuffed capsicums and onions on a platter with the tamarind sauce on the side.

I am sure you have had a variety of stuffed vegetables but have you ever eaten a stuffed onion? Try it, and you'll be surprised by how delicious it can be!

> Many of my non-vegetarian friends are fooled by these vegetarian *shami* kebabs made of Bengal gram!

KALE CHANE KE SHAMI KEBAB AUR DHANIAWALI TAMATAR KI CHUTNEY

Bengal Gram Kebabs with Tomato Coriander Chutney

Pankaj Bhadouria

Preparation Time: 30 minutes plus soaking
Cooking Time: 30 minutes
Serves: 4

Shami Kebab

Ingredients

Bengal gram (*kala chana*)	500 g
Onions, chopped	4 medium
Garlic, peeled	12-15 cloves
Ginger, chopped	2 inches
Salt	1 tsp
Lemon juice	2 tbsp

Method

- Soak the Bengal gram overnight.
- Tie the ingredients for the spice mix in a piece of muslin, or place in a spice infuser.
- Put the soaked gram into a pressure cooker with water reaching an inch above the gram. Add the chopped onions, garlic, ginger,

Coriander leaves, chopped	¼ cup
Red chilli powder	1 tsp
Garam masala powder	1 tsp
Vegetable oil	½ cup

Spice mix

Cloves	5
Bay leaves	2
Cinnamon	3-4 x 1-inch sticks
Black cardamoms	4-5
Green cardamoms	5
Nutmeg powder	¼ tsp
Cumin seeds	1 tsp
Dried red chillies	8
Black peppercorns	2 tbsp

Stuffing

Onions, finely chopped	3 medium
Green chillies, finely chopped	10
Ginger, finely chopped	1 inch
Green unripe mangoes, finely chopped	125 g
Mint leaves	¼ cup
Salt	¼ tsp

To serve

Sliced onions

salt and the spice bag and pressure cook for 15 minutes or till tender. Drain and reserve the cooking liquid.

- Remove the spice bag and grind the spices with a little of the cooking water to a fine paste. Grind the cooked gram using a little of the remaining water.

- Add the ground spice paste, lemon juice, chopped coriander, chilli powder and *garam masala* to the paste. Mix well and adjust seasoning.

- For the stuffing, mix together the chopped onions, green chillies, ginger, unripe mangoes and mint.

- Divide the gram mixture into 15-16 parts. Shape each one into a patty on your palm. Place a little stuffing in the centre of each patty and bring the edges together to enclose the stuffing.

- Heat the oil in a griddle or *tawa*. Place the patties on the griddle and cook over medium heat till nicely crisp on the underside. Flip the patties over and cook the other side as well.

Tamatar ki Chutney

Ingredients

Ripe tomatoes, chopped	2 large
Onion, chopped	1 large
Ginger, chopped	2 inches
Green chillies, chopped	3-4
Black salt	½ tsp
A few sprigs of fresh coriander	
Lemon juice	1 tsp

Method

- Process all the ingredients in a blender to make a purée. Add the lemon juice and mix well. Transfer to a bowl.

To serve: Arrange the kebabs on a platter, garnish with the onion rings and serve a bowl of tomato-coriander chutney on the side.

MUSHROOM AND CHEESE RAVIOLI IN SPICY PUMPKIN SAUCE

Pankaj Bhadouria

Preparation Time: 40 minutes
Cooking Time: 20 minutes
Serves: 4

Ingredients

Mushroom stuffing

Butter	1 tbsp
Fresh button mushrooms, finely chopped	100 g
Processed cheddar cheese, grated	100 g
Dried basil	½ tsp
Salt	¼ tsp
Black pepper powder	¼ tsp

Ravioli

Refined flour (*maida*)	400 g
Eggs	4
Salt	¼ tsp

Pumpkin sauce

Garlic, chopped	6 cloves
Yellow pumpkin, roughly chopped	500 g
Onions, chopped	2 large
Salt	1 tsp
Black pepper powder	1 tsp
Paprika	1 tsp
Fresh cream	½ cup

To serve

Deep-fried basil

Deep-fried chopped garlic

Method

For the mushroom stuffing

- Heat the butter in a pan and sauté the mushrooms. Add the remaining ingredients, mix well and remove from the heat.

For the ravioli

- Mix all the ingredients together to make a stiff dough. Do not add any water. If the dough seems too stiff, wet your hands and knead again. Wrap the dough in cling film and set aside for 10 minutes.

- Roll out the dough into a 12 x 16-inch rectangle and cut into 6 two-inch wide strips.

- Place a spoonful of the stuffing at 2-inch distances along half the strips. Moisten the strips between the filling. Place the reserved strips on top of the ones with the filling. Press down lightly around the filling to seal well. Cut into squares with the filling in the centre.

- Bring a large pan of water to a boil with 1 teaspoon salt. Add the ravioli and cook till almost done, taking care not to overcook the pasta. Drain and keep warm.

For the pumpkin sauce

- Dry-roast the garlic in a pan till golden brown.

- In another pan, cook the pumpkin and onion in 2 cups water, covered, for 15 minutes. Remove from the heat and leave to cool for a few minutes. Purée the pumpkin in a blender.

- Return the purée to the pan and add the salt, pepper, paprika and the roasted garlic.

- Bring to a boil and cook on a low heat for a few minutes. Stir in the cream and remove from the heat.

To serve: Pour the sauce into individual soup plates. Place a few ravioli on top and garnish with a sprinkling of deep-fried basil and garlic.

Pasta is a hot favourite all over the world. Macaroni has invaded practically every Indian kitchen by now. Here is a fresh pasta with a spicy sauce that will win over one and all. Remember, pasta is always cooked *al dente*. It should have a slight bite to it, and not be soft and mushy.

Parmigiana literally means cooked with parmesan cheese. And this dish of layered cheese and vegetables is the pride of Sicily and southern Italy.

VEGETABLE PARMIGIANA

Pankaj Bhadouria

Preparation Time: 30 minutes
Cooking Time: 30 minutes
Serves: 4

Ingredients

Brinjal	1 large
Zucchini	2
Salt	½ tsp
Black pepper powder	½ tsp
Fresh breadcrumbs	1 cup
Oil	3½ tbsp
Tomato sauce	1 cup
Cheddar cheese, grated	100 g
Parmesan cheese, grated	100 g
Fresh basil leaves, chopped	10

Tomato sauce

Olive oil	1 tbsp
Onion, finely chopped	1 medium
Garlic, finely chopped	4 cloves
Fresh chopped thyme OR	1 tbsp
Dried thyme	2 tsp
Carrot, finely chopped	1 medium
Tomato purée	1¼ cups
Salt	½ tsp
Crushed peppercorns	1 tsp
Bay leaves	2

To serve

Bread rolls

Method

- Preheat an oven to 200°C/400°F/Gas 6.

- Cut the vegetables lengthways into thin long strips. Season lightly with salt and pepper. Coat the strips with the breadcrumbs.

- Place the vegetable strips on a greased baking sheet in the oven and cook till crisp. Alternatively, deep-fry till crisp. Remove and set aside to cool.

- For the tomato sauce, heat the oil in a pan and sauté the onion and garlic till light brown. Add the thyme and carrot and 1 cup water, and cook till the carrot is tender. Add the tomato purée, salt, pepper and bay leaf. Bring to a boil, lower the heat and simmer for 15 minutes till the sauce is thick.

- To assemble the dish, in a 6-inch square or round baking dish, place a third of the 2 vegetable strips alternately side by side.

- Cover with a layer of tomato sauce. Mix both cheeses together and sprinkle half the mixture over the sauce together with half the chopped basil. Top with another third of the vegetables and repeat the cheese, sauce and basil layers.

- Add the final layer of vegetables, sprinkle breadcrumbs on top and bake in the preheated oven for about 8-10 minutes till the cheese melts.

To serve: Cut into squares or wedges and serve with warm bread rolls.

VEGETABLES AU GRATIN WITH HERB AND ONION QUICK BREAD

Pankaj Bhadouria

Preparation Time: 30 minutes
Cooking Time: 40 minutes
Serves: 4

Vegetables au Gratin

Ingredients

Broccoli florets	250 g
Cauliflower florets	250 g
Cheese Sauce	
Butter	2 tbsp
Refined flour (*maida*)	2 tbsp
Milk	1 ½ cups
Cream	1 cup
Salt	1 tsp
Crushed black pepper	1 tsp
Dried chilli flakes	½ tsp
Dried thyme	1 tsp
Cheddar cheese, grated	100 g

Method

• Blanch the broccoli and the cauliflower florets for 3-4 minutes in boiling water. Drain and refresh in cold water. Place in a colander to drain.

• For the cheese sauce, melt the butter in a pan. Add the flour and cook for 1 minute. Gradually add the milk, stirring vigorously to prevent any lumps from being formed.

• Cook on a low heat till the sauce starts to thicken. Remove and stir in the cream, salt, pepper and mixed herbs.

• Add half the cheese and stir to mix. Return to the heat and cook for another minute to allow the cheese to melt.

• Preheat an oven to 180°C/350°F/Gas 4.

• Arrange the cauliflower and broccoli florets in a 6-inch square or round ovenproof dish. Pour the sauce over the vegetables. Cover with the remaining grated cheese. Bake in the preheated oven for 10-12 minutes till the cheese melts and is bubbly on top.

• Alternatively, the entire amount of cheese may be added to the sauce and the vegetables cooked in it for 5-6 minutes till tender yet firm.

Herb and Onion Quick Bread

Ingredients

Refined flour (*maida*)	250 g
Baking powder	1 tsp
Salt	1 tsp
Egg	1
Sugar	1 tbsp

Method

• Preheat an oven to 180°C/350°F/Gas 4.

• Sift the flour and baking powder together into a bowl. Add the salt, egg and sugar to the milk and stir to mix.

• Pour the milk mixture into the flour and mix to make a soft, slack dough. Do not knead the dough.

Milk	1 cup
Italian mixed dried herbs	1 tsp
Vegetable oil	2-3 tbsp
Onions, finely sliced	2 large

- Grease a deep 8-inch loaf tin with some of the oil. Spread the dough in the tin and sprinkle the herbs on the top.

- Sauté the onions lightly in a pan in 1 tablespoon oil. Sprinkle over the top of the dough.

- Place the tin in the preheated oven and bake for 20 minutes, or till the bread is risen and the top is a light golden brown. Cool and cut into slices. Serve warm.

To serve: Place portions of the baked vegetables on a plate and serve with slices of the warm bread.

Au gratin - this was one of the first baked dishes that I learned to cook. It is still as delicious today as it was then!

You can stuff the pea and corn filling into squares of phyllo pastry, spring roll or wonton sheets to make small bags. Bake or deep-fry till crisp.

GREEN PEA AND CORN PARCELS WITH STIR-FRIED CAULIFLOWER AND POTATOES

Chef Ajay Chopra

Preparation Time: 25 minutes
Cooking Time: 35 minutes
Serves: 4

Green Pea and Corn Parcels

Ingredients

Frozen peas	350 g
Ginger, chopped	2 inches
Green chillies, chopped	5
Ghee	2 tbsp
Cumin seeds	1 tbsp
A pinch of asafoetida (hing)	

Method

- Put the peas, ginger and green chillies into a blender and blend to a fine paste, adding a little water if necessary.

- Heat the ghee in large pan or wok and add the cumin seeds. When they begin to change colour, add the asafoetida, followed by the green pea paste. Stir over a low heat for about 12-15 minutes, until the moisture has evaporated and the mixture attains a soft, doughy consistency.

Drained tinned sweet corn kernels	¼ cup
Salt	1½ tsp
Garam masala	1 tsp
Sugar	½ tsp
Finely chopped fresh coriander	2 tbsp
1x 250 g packet phyllo pastry or 8 packaged spring roll sheets	
Melted butter, for brushing	2 tbsp

- Add the sweet corn and cook for a couple of minutes longer. Stir in the salt and *garam masala* and adjust the seasoning. Cook for another 3 minutes, stir in the sugar and remove from heat. Mix in the chopped coriander and leave to cool.

- Preheat an oven to 200°C/400°F/Gas 6.

- Lay out a sheet of phyllo pastry on a work surface and brush with the melted butter. Cover with a second sheet and then cut the double sheet into 4 equal parts. Place a quarter of the cooled pea and corn mixture in the centre of each piece of pastry, fold over the top and bottom of the pastry, then tuck the sides underneath.

- Place on a well-greased baking tray, brush with melted butter and bake in the preheated oven for 8 to 10 minutes till crisp and golden.

Stir-Fried Cauliflower and Potatoes

Ingredients

Vegetable or corn oil	1 tbsp
Cumin seeds	½ tsp
Onion, finely chopped	1 small
Potatoes, cut into wedges	2 large
Turmeric powder	½ tsp
Salt	1 tsp
Red chilli powder	½ tsp
Cumin powder	½ tsp
Cauliflower florets	150 g
Tomato, seeded and sliced	1
Garam masala	1 tsp
Finely chopped fresh coriander	1 tbsp
Lemon juice	4 tsp

Method

- Heat the oil in a large pan and add the cumin seeds. When they begin to change colour, add the onion and sauté until golden.

- Add the potatoes and cook for 3 minutes, covering the pan with a lid to allow the potatoes to cook in their own steam.

- Add the turmeric, salt, chilli powder and cumin powder and sauté for 2 to 3 minutes. Add the cauliflower and cover the pan again. Reduce the heat to minimum and let the vegetables cook in their own juices for about 5 minutes.

- Sprinkle with a little water, if necessary, and cook for a couple more minutes till the vegetables are tender.

- Mix in the tomato and stir-fry. Sprinkle with the *garam masala*, chopped coriander and lemon juice.

To serve: Arrange the pea and corn parcels on a plate and serve the stir-fried cauliflower and potatoes on the side. Garnish with fresh coriander.

KER SANGRI

Rajasthani Dried Desert Berries and Beans in
a Spicy Tomato Yoghurt Sauce

Chef Ajay Chopra

Preparation Time: 15 minutes + soaking
Cooking Time: 20 minutes
Serves: 4

Ingredients

Dried desert berries (*ker*)	25 g
Dried desert beans (*sangri*)	75 g
Mustard oil	1 tbsp
Ghee	1 tbsp
Cumin seeds	1 tsp
Dried red chilli	1 large
Chopped garlic	1 tbsp
Onion, finely chopped	1 large
Cumin powder	½ tsp
Coriander powder	½ tsp
Turmeric powder	1 tsp
Red chilli powder	1 tsp
Tomatoes, finely chopped	2 large
Kumita seeds*, rinsed	25 g
Salt	1 tsp
Plain yoghurt	6 tbsp
Finely chopped coriander	1 tbsp
A pinch of sugar	
Lemon juice	2 tsp

To serve

Fried *papad*

Roti

*Kumita is a desert berry grown in Rajasthan.

Method

- Wash and soak the *ker* and *sangri*, separately, in cold water to cover for 3 hours. Drain.

- Heat the mustard oil in a large pan until it reaches smoking point, and add the ghee. When the ghee melts, add the cumin seeds and red chilli and sauté till the seeds start to change colour. Add the chopped garlic and sauté for a few seconds.

- Add the chopped onion and sauté until golden brown; add the cumin, coriander, turmeric and chilli powders and sauté for a minute. Add the tomatoes and cook until the moisture from the tomatoes has evaporated and oil starts to separate from the mixture.

- Add the *ker*, *sangri*, and *kumita* seeds and sauté for a couple of minutes.

- Add the salt and yoghurt and stir until the mixture returns to a slow boil. Pour in half a cup of hot water and cook, stirring occasionally, for 10 -15 minutes, until the beans and berries have almost doubled in size, and have soaked up most of the liquid from the sauce.

- Stir in the chopped coriander, sugar and lemon juice.

To serve: Ladle the *ker sangri* into a bowl and serve with crisp *papad* and hot *roti*.

Legend has it that these dried berries and beans once saved a famine-ridden population from starvation in the hot desert. From then on the two desert companions have come together in an iconic Rajasthani dish, which is a personal favourite.

In India, a minced chicken kebab is known as a *reshmi* kebab because of its silky, smooth texture. This classic dish has been given a twist by adding corn to provide a more interesting texture. You can also barbecue the kebabs, cook them in a *tandoor* or on a *tawa*.

MURGH MAKKAI SEEKH KEBAB

Minced Chicken and Corn Kebabs

Chef Ajay Chopra

Preparation Time: 30 minutes
Cooking Time: 25 minutes
Serves: 4

Ingredients

Minced chicken	600 g
Ginger, chopped	1 inch
Garlic, chopped	2 cloves
Green chillies, chopped	3 small
Finely chopped coriander	3 tbsp
Crushed black peppercorns	½ tsp
Mace (*javitri*) powder	1 tsp
Cardamom powder	1 tsp
Salt	1 tsp
Grated processed cheddar cheese	3 tbsp
Drained tinned sweet corn kernels	100 g
Melted butter or oil, for basting	3 tbsp
Lemon juice	4 tsp
Chaat masala (optional)	½ tsp

To serve

Finely chopped coriander

Naan

Thinly sliced radish

Method

- Put the minced chicken into a bowl and mix together with the ginger, garlic, green chillies, coriander, crushed pepper, mace and cardamom powders and salt.

- Process in a blender, or knead the mixture well with your hands. Place in a refrigerator to chill for 2-3 hours. Mix in the cheese and sweet corn and divide the mixture into 4 portions.

- Shape each portion around a metal skewer, squeezing the meat gently with wet hands so the mixture adheres to the skewer.

- Cook under a very hot grill or on a grill pan for 10-12 minutes, brushing frequently with butter or oil and turning the skewers to ensure that the kebabs cook evenly on all sides.

- Sprinkle with lemon juice and *chaat masala*, and serve immediately.

To serve: Sprinkle the hot kebabs with finely chopped coriander and serve with *naan* and sliced radish.

SPICE-ENCRUSTED POMFRET WITH TOMATO AND LEMON SAUCE

Chef Ajay Chopra

Preparation Time: 30 minutes
Cooking Time: 20 minutes
Serves: 4

Ingredients

Pomfret	1 whole (800 g)
Vegetable or corn oil	1 tbsp
First marinade	
Ginger paste	½ tsp
Garlic paste	½ tsp
White pepper powder	½ tsp
Salt	¼ tsp
Second marinade	
Grated processed cheddar cheese	1 tbsp
Yoghurt	2 tbsp
Ginger, finely chopped	2 inches
Green chillies, finely chopped	2 small
Finely chopped fresh coriander	½ tbsp
Salt	½ tsp
Cream	1 tbsp
Spice mix	
Coriander seeds	½ tsp
Cumin seeds	½ tsp
Black peppercorns,	½ tsp
Dried red chilli	1 large
Tomato and lemon sauce	
Ghee	100 g
Bay leaf (*tej patta*)	1
Fresh tomato purée	½ cup
Ginger paste	1 tsp
Garlic paste	1 tsp
Red chilli powder	1 tsp
Cumin powder	1 tsp
Coconut milk	1½ cups
Salt	¼ tsp
Sugar	¼ tsp
Fresh lemon leaves OR	4
Lemon grass stalks, lightly crushed	2
To serve	
Steamed rice	

Method

For the Fish

- Wash, clean and slice the pomfret on the bone. Mix together all the ingredients for the first marinade, rub over the fish and set aside for 20 minutes.

- For the second marinade, put the cheese into a small bowl and rub it into a paste with your fingers (add a teaspoon of flour to prevent lumps forming). Add the yoghurt and mix to a smooth paste. Add the rest of the ingredients, stirring in the cream at the end.

- Roast all the ingredients for the spice mix in a dry frying pan and crush them coarsely with a pestle and mortar.

- Preheat an oven to 200°C/400°F/Gas 6.

- Heat the oil in a large ovenproof frying pan. Add the fish and sear the slices on both sides. Spread the second marinade over the fish, and sprinkle with the roasted spice. Transfer to the preheated oven and cook for about 10 minutes, until the fish is tender.

For the tomato and lemon sauce

- Heat the ghee or butter in a pan; add the bay leaf and tomato purée and cook on a low heat for 5 minutes.

- In a bowl, mix together the ginger and garlic pastes, chilli powder and cumin powder with a little water to make a smooth paste. Add to the pan and cook over a low heat for 5 minutes, stirring continuously to prevent the paste from sticking to the bottom of the pan.

- Stir in the coconut milk and simmer for 5 minutes, until the sauce turns glossy. Add the salt, sugar and lemon leaves or lemon grass and cook for another 3-4 minutes, until the sauce is infused with the lemon flavour.

To serve: Arrange the fish slices in a dish and pour the sauce over. Serve with steamed rice.

The cheese and yoghurt marinade keeps the pomfret moist and succulent while cooking. The delicately-flavoured lemon sauce provides a clean, light contrast to the meaty texture of the fish.

Bring home some asparagus the next time you go vegetable shopping, and try out this delightful combination of crunchy cumin-flavoured asparagus on a soft bed of traditionally-spiced aubergine.

STIR-FRIED ASPARAGUS WITH BENGALI-STYLE ROASTED AUBERGINE

Chef Ajay Chopra

Preparation Time: 30 minutes
Cooking Time: 15 minutes
Serves: 4

Ingredients

Roasted aubergine

Aubergine (brinjal)	1 large (200 g)
Oil, for brushing	1 tbsp
Red onion, finely chopped	1 large
Green chilli, finely chopped	½ inch
Mustard oil	1 tbsp
Salt	½ tsp
Finely chopped coriander	1 tbsp

Stir-fried asparagus

Vegetable or corn oil	2 tbsp
Cumin seeds	1 tsp
Onion, finely chopped	1 large
Red chilli powder	1 tsp
Tomato, chopped	1
Asparagus spears (*shatwar*), trimmed and peeled	20
Salt	1 tsp
Ginger, finely chopped	1 inch
Fresh coriander, finely chopped	1 tbsp
Lemon juice	2 tsp
Garam masala	½ tbsp

To serve

Fresh red chillies, sliced	2

Method

For the roasted aubergine

- Preheat an oven to 200°C/ 400°F/Gas 6.

- Brush the aubergine with oil, place on a baking tray and roast it in the oven for about 20 minutes until soft. Remove from the oven and leave until cool enough to handle, then peel off the skin and chop up the pulp.

- Mix in all the remaining ingredients and keep warm.

For the asparagus

- Heat the oil in a large wok or frying pan and add the cumin seeds. When they begin to change colour, add the onion and sauté until golden brown.

- Add the chilli powder and sauté for 30 seconds. Add the tomato and cook until soft.

- Add the asparagus and toss well to mix; add the salt. Cook for 2-3 minutes, until the asparagus is just tender.

- Sprinkle the chopped ginger and coriander over the asparagus, followed by the lemon juice and *garam masala*.

To serve: Spoon the roasted aubergine into a dish and arrange the asparagus on top, garnished with sliced red chillies.

BATAER KA KORMA

Quails in an Aromatic Spiced Cashew Nut Sauce

Chef Kunal Kapoor

Preparation Time: 35 minutes
Cooking Time: 35 minutes
Serves: 4

Ingredients

Quails (*bataer*)	500 g
Salt	1½ tsp
Oil	¾ cup
Green cardamoms	8
Black cumin seeds (*shahi jeera*)	1 tbsp
Cinnamon	2-inch stick
Cloves	5
Bay leaf (*tej patta*)	1
Ginger paste	100 g
Garlic paste	100 g
Turmeric powder	2 tsp
Yellow chilli powder	2 tsp
Red chilli powder	2 tsp
Coriander powder	2 tbsp
Yogurt, whisked	1 cup
Brown onion paste*	150 g
Brown cashew nut paste **	75 g
Screw pine (*kewra*) water	2 tsp
Rose water	2 tsp
Mace (*javitri*) powder	1 tsp
Green cardamom powder	1 tsp

To serve

Steamed rice

Naan or *roti*

* To make 150 g brown onion paste, slice 350 g onions and deep-fry till golden brown. Purée in a blender till smooth.

** To make 75 g brown cashew nut paste, fry 50 g cashew nuts in oil till brown. Grind to a paste.

Method

- Clean the quails, rub all over with 1 teaspoon salt and leave to marinate for 15 minutes.

- Heat the oil in a thick-bottomed pan. Add the cardamoms, black cumin, cinnamon, cloves and bay leaf. When the spices begin to sizzle, add the ginger and garlic pastes.

- Mix each of the following separately in a little water: ½ teaspoon salt, turmeric, yellow chilli powder, red chilli powder and coriander powder. Add one after the other to the pan and cook till the oil separates from the paste.

- Increase the heat and pour in the whisked yogurt, stirring continuously till it comes to a boil. Reduce the heat and simmer till the oil rises to the surface.

- Add the quails and cook with a little water, if required, till half done. Add the brown onion paste and stir well till blended. Add 3 cups water and bring to a boil and cook till the gravy thickens.

- Take the pan off the heat and remove the quails with a slotted spoon. Strain the sauce into a pan. Return the strained sauce to the heat and add the cashew nut paste, *kewra* water, rose water, mace and green cardamom powders.

- Gently lower the quails into the sauce and cook on a low heat for one minute. Adjust the seasoning and serve hot.

To serve: Arrange the *bataer* in a serving dish and pour the sauce on top. Serve with steamed rice, *naan* or *roti*.

A favourite of the Mughal aristocracy, and once described by the British as 'flying pats of butter', quails are especially delicious steeped in this rich, creamy spiced sauce.

The invention of this iconic mutton dish is attributed to the legendary Lahori chef Beli Ram, who is believed to have cooked it for Maharaja Ranjit Singh. Slow cooking in yoghurt is the secret of the tender, succulent mutton enrobed in a thick, flavourful sauce.

GOSHT BELI RAM

Mutton Stewed in Yoghurt and Spices

Chef Kunal Kapoor

Preparation Time: 30 minutes
Cooking Time: 30 minutes
Serves: 4

Ingredients

Ingredient	Amount
Mutton on the bone, chopped	500 g
Salt	½ tsp
Ginger paste	100 g
Garlic paste	100 g
Turmeric powder	2 tsp
Coriander powder	2 tbsp
Cumin powder	1 tbsp
Red chilli powder	2 tsp
Dried fenugreek leaf (*kasoori methi*) powder	2 tsp
Onions, sliced	2 large
Onions, sliced and fried till brown	2 large
Coriander seeds, pounded	2 tbsp
Black peppercorns, freshly ground	1 tbsp
Yoghurt, whisked	2 cups
Green chillies, chopped	2 small
Oil	1 cup
Finely chopped coriander	1 tbsp

To serve

Fried sliced onions

Chapatti

Method

- Place the mutton in a thick-bottomed pan. Add the rest of the ingredients and mix well. Leave to marinate for 10 minutes.
- Place the pan on a high heat and bring to a boil. Reduce the heat and simmer, covered, till the meat is tender.

To serve: Transfer the mutton to a dish, garnish with fried onion slices and serve with hot *chapatti*.

GRILLED COTTAGE CHEESE WITH ROASTED PEPPER CHUTNEY

Chef Kunal Kapoor

Preparation Time: 20 minutes
Cooking Time: 15 minutes
Serves: 4

Grilled Cottage Cheese

Ingredients

Cottage cheese (*paneer*)	250 g
Salt	½ tsp
Turmeric powder	3 tsp
Ginger paste	2 tsp
Garlic paste	2 tsp
Mustard oil	4 tbsp
Gram flour	4 tbsp
Juice of 1 lemon	
Red chilli flakes	3 tsp
Finely chopped garlic	2 tbsp
Yellow chilli powder	2 tsp
Finely chopped coriander	2 tbsp
Black pepper powder	1 tsp
To serve	
Chaat masala	1 tsp
Green salad	

Method

* Cut the cottage cheese into 3-inch long fingers.

* Sprinkle with a mixture of the salt, half the turmeric powder and the ginger and garlic pastes. Set aside in a warm place to marinate for half an hour. Drain the water that is given out and set aside.

* Heat 3 tablespoons mustard oil in a pan and add the gram flour. Sauté on a low heat till it browns slightly. Remove from the heat and stir in the remaining turmeric powder and set aside to cool.

* Add the lemon juice, chilli flakes, chopped garlic, yellow chilli powder, chopped coriander, pepper and salt to taste. Marinate the cottage cheese in the mixture for 15 minutes.

* Heat a frying pan and add 1 tablespoon oil. Add the cottage cheese and cook till brown on all sides. Remove and set aside.

Roasted Pepper Chutney

Ingredients

Tomatoes	3 large
Green pepper (capsicum)	1 large
Red pepper (capsicum)	1 large
Onion, finely chopped	1 large
A few sprigs of fresh coriander, finely chopped	
Green chilli, finely chopped	1
Juice of 1 lemon	
Salt	½ tsp
Crushed black peppercorns	1 tsp

Method

* Purée the tomatoes in a blender and transfer to a bowl.

* Roast both the peppers on an open flame till charred on all sides. Dip in water and remove the skin. Dice the peppers and add to the tomato purée.

* Add the chopped onion, coriander and chilli and stir to mix. Add the lemon juice, salt and pepper and mix well.

To serve: Stack the *paneer* fingers one on top of the other, sprinkle *chaat masala* and serve with fresh green salad and the roasted pepper chutney.

The ubiquitous *paneer tikka* is showcased here with a colourful, smoky pepper chutney.

Potli masala is an aromatic blend of spices and dried herbs which perfume a dish with an exotic fragrance and flavour. The spices are usually tied in a piece of muslin and the bundle (*potli*) immersed in the gravy or stock while cooking. Sprinkle more *potli masala* on the kebabs for a stronger aroma.

SUBZ KHATAI KEBAB

Aromatic Smoked Vegetable Kebabs

Chef Kunal Kapoor

Preparation Time: 30 minutes
Cooking Time: 30 minutes
Serves: 4

Ingredients

A pinch of saffron	
Yam (*jimikand*)	600 g
Ridged gourd (*turai*)	100 g
Split Bengal gram (*chana dal*)	¼ cup
Ginger paste	3 tbsp
Garlic paste	3 tbsp
Green chilli paste	2 tsp
Salt	1 tsp
Onion, ground to a paste	1 small
Brown onion paste*	100 g
Brown cashew nut paste**	50 g
Yellow chilli powder	2 tsp
Red chilli powder	2 tsp
Potli Masala (recipe below)	2 tbsp
Screw pine (*kewra*) water	2 tsp
Rose water	2 tsp
Meetha ittar***	1 drop
Roasted dried split Bengal gram (*daria dal*) powder	3 tbsp
A piece of charcoal	
Cloves	4
Ghee	1 tbsp

To serve

Green Chutney (page 33)

Method

- Lightly crush the saffron with a wooden pestle. Add 2 tablespoons warm water and set aside.

- Peel and boil the yam and ridged gourd till soft and tender. Separately wash and boil the *chana dal*. Cool and process with the boiled vegetables in a blender without adding any water. Transfer to a large bowl and add the ginger paste, garlic paste, green chilli paste, salt and raw onion paste. Set aside for 10 minutes.

- Add the brown onion paste, brown cashew nut paste, yellow chilli and red chilli powders. Sprinkle the *potli masala*, *kewra* and rose waters and *meetha ittar*. Add the soaked saffron and roasted *daria dal* powder.

- Make a well in the centre of the mixture and place a burning piece of charcoal in it. Place the cloves on top of the charcoal and pour the ghee over. Immediately cover the bowl with a tight-fitting lid. This is an ancient Indian way of smoking called *dhungar*. Set aside for 20 minutes. Remove the lid and the piece of charcoal.

- Shape the mixture with wet hands into round patties (kebabs).

- Heat the ghee in a *tawa* or frying pan and shallow-fry the kebabs till golden.

* To make 100 g brown onion paste, slice 250 g onions and deep-fry till golden brown. Purée in a blender till smooth

** To make 50 g brown cashew nut paste, fry 30 g cashew nuts in oil till brown. Grind to a paste.

*** *Meetha ittar* is available in shops selling Lucknowi or Hyderabadi spices.

To serve: Arrange the kebabs on a platter and serve with green chutney.

Potli Masala

Grind or pound together 1tbsp dried rose petals, 1 tbsp black cumin seeds (*shahi jeera*), 2 bay leaves (*tej pata*), 30 g dried galangal (*paan ki jad*), ¾ tsp mace (*javitri*), 2 tsp green cardamoms (*chhoti elaichi*), 4 g vetiver roots (*khus ki jad*), 10 g sandalwood powder (*chandan burada*).

SHATWAR AUR PUDINA KA SHORBA

Velvety Asparagus and Mint Soup

Chef Kunal Kapoor

Preparation Time: 20 minutes
Cooking Time: 10 minutes
Serves: 4

Ingredients

Tender green asparagus (*shatwar*)	400 g
Butter	100 g
Bay leaf (*tej patta*)	1
Black peppercorns	10
Cumin seeds	2 tsp
Onions, finely chopped	2 large
Garlic, finely chopped	8-10 cloves
Refined flour (*maida*)	4 tbsp
Fresh mint leaves	½ cup
Salt	½ tsp
A pinch of nutmeg	

To serve

Coarsely crushed peppercorns
Curls of butter

Method

- Wash the asparagus and chop roughly.

- Heat the butter in a pan and add the bay leaf, peppercorns and cumin seeds. When the seeds begin to change colour, add the chopped onions and garlic and sauté for a few seconds. Add the asparagus and toss to mix.

- Reduce the heat and add the flour; sauté for a minute and quickly add 1 cup water. Bring to a boil, stirring continuously, and remove from the heat.

- Transfer the mixture into a blender along with the mint leaves and blend to a smooth purée.

- Strain into the pan and return to the heat. Add salt, remove from heat and sprinkle with nutmeg.

To serve: Ladle the hot *shorba* into bowls and garnish with crushed peppercorns and curls of butter.

The colour of the soup should be a pale green. Make sure you don't boil the soup on high heat while reheating it or the colour will darken. You can also stir in a tablespoon of cream just before serving.

Desserts

People have a sweet tooth but God has given me 32 sweet teeth! This is one of those recipes which has all 32 of them craving for more.

BAKLAVA

Pankaj Bhadouria

Preparation Time: 60 minutes
Cooking Time: 60 minutes
Serves: 8

Ingredients

Phyllo pastry*

Refined flour (*maida*)	450 g
Vinegar	1 tbsp
Oil	1 tsp
Lemon juice	1 tsp
Hot water	1 cup
Butter	200 g

Filling

Mixed nuts (walnuts, pistachios, almonds), finely chopped	450 g
Cinnamon powder	1 tsp

Syrup

Water	1 cup
Caster sugar	½ cup
Honey	½ cup
Vanilla essence	1 tsp

To serve

Sugar syrup

Pistachio flakes

Honey (optional)

*Commercial phyllo pastry is made by machines to create a texture that is very difficult to achieve by hand. Use 450 g of readymade phyllo dough for this recipe.

Method

- For the phyllo pastry, place half the flour in a bowl and mix in the vinegar, oil, lemon juice and hot water. Knead the dough on a floured surface till it is stiff. Divide the dough into 20 parts.

- Roll out each part into a very thin, almost translucent sheet, like a *roomali roti*. Cut into an 8-inch square, cover with a damp cloth and set aside.

- If using a pasta machine, pass the dough through the machine till you reach mark 1. Dust with flour several times. Cut into 8-inch squares and cover with a damp cloth.

- For the filling, in a bowl, toss the chopped nuts with cinnamon. Set aside.

- For the syrup, in a pan, heat together the water, sugar, honey and vanilla. Bring to a boil, lower the heat and simmer for 20 minutes.

- Preheat the oven to 170°C/325°F/Gas 3.

- To assemble the baklava, butter the base and sides of an 8-inch square baking tin.

- Spread two sheets of pastry on the base of the tin one on top of the other. Brush with melted butter, then add 2 more sheets. Repeat till you have about 8 layers of butter and pastry. Sprinkle 2 to 3 spoonfuls of the nut mixture on top. Repeat the layers of pastry, butter and nuts. Use a sharp knife and cut the pastry into squares or diamond shapes while still in the tin.

- Bake in the preheated oven for 1 hour, or till the pastry is crisp.

- Remove from the oven and pour the prepared sugar syrup all over the baklava; sprinkle with pistachio flakes. Set aside to cool.

To serve: Arrange pieces of baklava on a plate. Drizzle with more sugar syrup and sprinkle pistachio slivers. For extra sweetness add some honey as well!

CHOCOLATE LAVA CAKES

Pankaj Bhadouria

Preparation Time: 20 minutes
Cooking Time: 10 minutes
Serves: 6 small cakes

Ingredients

Butter	75 g
Dark chocolate	100 g
Eggs	2 extra-large
Egg yolk	1
Sugar	3 tbsp
Refined flour (*maida*)	3 tbsp
Cocoa powder	2 tsp
Salt	¼ tsp
Icing sugar	½ cup

Method

- Preheat the oven to 180°C/350°F/Gas 4.
- Melt the butter and chocolate together over a low heat.
- In a bowl, whisk the eggs, egg yolk and sugar lightly till the sugar has dissolved. Pour the melted chocolate mixture into the egg mix and stir well.
- Sift the flour, cocoa powder and baking powder together. Fold the flour mixture into the egg mixture quickly. Do not overmix as this will make the cake heavy.
- Pour the batter into 6 buttered ramekins or small ovenproof dishes. Bake in the preheated oven for 10 minutes. Remove from the oven.

To serve: Dust icing sugar through a sieve on top of each cake and serve immediately, either in the ramekins or turned out onto plates.

Kids are going to thank me for this recipe! My children love lava cake and demand one every time we go out for pizzas. So every time I make pizza at home, this has to be made as well!

Oooh! The aroma of a cinnamon-flavoured apple pie baking in the oven is one of the most heavenly smells in the world!

APPLE CINNAMON TART

Pankaj Bhadouria

Preparation Time: 20 minutes
Cooking Time: 45 minutes
Serves: 4

Ingredients

Pastry

Refined flour (*maida*)	175 g
A pinch of salt	
Chilled butter	85 g
Caster sugar	2 tbsp
Egg yolk	1

Filling

Crisp apples	8
Lemon juice	1 tbsp
Caster sugar	6 tbsp
Butter	2 tbsp
Cinnamon powder	½ tsp
Apricot jam	5 tbsp

To serve

Vanilla ice cream

Method

- For the pastry, sift the flour into a bowl with the salt. Rub the butter in lightly with your fingertips till the mixture resembles breadcrumbs.

- Stir in the sugar, egg yolk and 2 tablespoons water and knead gently to make a dough. Wrap in cling film and place in a refrigerator to chill for 30 minutes.

- For the filling, peel, core and chop 5 apples. Place in a pan and add half the lemon juice and 2 tablespoons water. Cover and cook over low heat for 15 minutes, stirring occasionally. Add half the sugar and the butter and cook for 2-3 minutes.

- Preheat the oven to 200°C/400°F/Gas 6. Roll out the chilled dough and use to line a 10-inch loose-bottomed or two 6-inch flan tins. Prick the base all over with a fork. Cover with greaseproof paper and fill with dried beans. Bake blind for 10 minutes. Remove the beans and paper and bake again for 5 minutes.

- Lower the oven setting to 180°C/350°F/Gas 4.

- Peel, core and thinly slice the remaining apples. Toss the slices with the remaining lemon juice and the sugar. Spread the cooked apple purée over the pastry base and arrange the apple slices on top. Sprinkle with the cinnamon powder.

- Bake for 30 minutes in the preheated oven until golden. Leave the tart to cool slightly and remove from the tin.

- Gently heat the jam with 2 tablespoons water and bring to a boil. Cook for another minute to thicken it.

- Pass the jam through a sieve and brush over the tart to glaze it.

To serve: Cut the tart into wedges and serve warm with dollops of vanilla ice cream.

COCONUT CARAMEL CUSTARD

Pankaj Bhadouria

Preparation Time: 10 minutes
Cooking Time: 30 minutes
Serves: 4

Ingredients

Eggs	3
Sugar	½ cup
Coconut milk	1 ½ cups
Cream	1 cup
Vanilla essence	½ tsp
Sugar for caramel	4 tbsp

To serve

Fresh coconut curls

Method

- In a bowl, whisk the eggs lightly with sugar till the sugar dissolves. Add the coconut milk, cream and essence and stir to mix.

- Prepare 4 heatproof moulds by putting in a spoonful of sugar. Hold the moulds with a pair of tongs over an open flame and let the sugar caramelise to a golden brown. Remove and allow to set.

- Pour the prepared custard into the moulds.

- Place the moulds in a pan with some water. Place the pan on the heat and bring the water to a boil. Reduce the heat and cook for 30 minutes, or till a skewer or the point of a thin knife inserted into the custard comes out clean. Remove the moulds from the pan and set aside to cool. Chill in a refrigerator.

To serve: Turn out the custards onto individual serving plates. Garnish with coconut curls for a special touch. Serve cold.

Coconut custard is a Thai dessert, to which I have added caramel to create a fusion of flavours.

110

This recipe calls for drained yoghurt instead of mascarpone cheese. Delicious!

MANGO CHEESECAKE

Pankaj Bhadouria

Preparation Time: 30 minutes + setting
Serves: 4

Ingredients

Marie biscuits	200 g
Melted butter	½ cup
Mango pulp	1½ cups
Sugar	½ cup
Drained (hung) yoghurt*	½ cup
Fresh cream	½ cup
Unflavoured gelatine	1 tbsp

To garnish

Fresh mango slices	6-8
Drinking chocolate	
Chocolate curls	

*Hang 250 g full fat yoghurt in a piece of muslin or cheesecloth over a bowl in the refrigerator, overnight or for at least 8 hours. Discard the whey.

Method

• Crush or process the biscuits to a fine powder. Transfer to a bowl and mix in the melted butter.

• Line the base of a 6-inch shallow pie dish evenly and smoothly with the biscuit mixture. Place in the freezer to set.

• Whisk the mango pulp, add the sugar, drained yoghurt and cream, and mix well to make a smooth mixture.

• Soak the gelatine in 2-3 tablespoons water in a small pan. Cook over a low heat to dissolve. Stir the gelatine into the mango mixture and pour over the set biscuit base.

• Cover and place in a refrigerator to set overnight, or for at least 6 hours.

To serve: Arrange slices of mango and chocolate curls on the cheesecake and dust lightly with drinking chocolate. Cut into wedges and serve.

111

An assortment of pretty cupcakes is sure to brighten up your table and lighten the mood of guests of all ages!

CUPCAKE FIESTA

Pankaj Bhadouria

Preparation Time: 15 minutes
Cooking Time: 20 minutes
Makes: 12

Basic Vanilla Cupcakes

Ingredients

Butter, softened	150 g
Caster sugar	150 g
Refined flour (*maida*)	175 g
Baking powder	½ tsp
Eggs, beaten	3
Vanilla essence	1 tsp

Method

• Preheat the oven to 180°C/350°F/Gas 4. Line a 12 cupcake tin with paper cases.

• Sift the flour and baking powder together twice.

• Place all the ingredients in a large bowl. Beat with an electric mixer for 2 minutes, until light and creamy.

• Divide the mixture evenly between the moulds.

• Bake in the preheated oven for 18-20 minutes until well-risen and firm to touch.

• Leave to cool for a few minutes and then transfer to a wire rack to cool completely. Decorate with icings below.

Variations:

Choco-Chip Cupcakes: Fold 2 tablespoons chocolate chips into the beaten mixture.

Chocolate Cupcakes: Add 1 tablespoon cocoa powder to the flour and baking powder and sift twice.

Icings

Royal Icing:

Ingredients

Egg white	1 large
Fresh lemon juice	1 tsp
Icing sugar, sifted	1½ cups

Method

• In the bowl of an electric mixer (or with a hand mixer), beat the egg whites with the lemon juice until combined.

• Add the sifted icing sugar and beat on low speed until combined and smooth.

• The icing needs to be used immediately or transferred to an airtight container, as royal icing hardens when exposed to air.

Butter Icing:

Ingredients:

Icing sugar	300 g
White unsalted butter	120 g
Vanilla essence	½ tsp
Food colour (optional)	

Method

- Sift the icing sugar to remove lumps.
- In a bowl, cream the butter till soft. Add the icing sugar, a little at a time, beating continuously.
- Add the vanilla essence and continue beating until the icing is creamy and fluffy. Add a few drops of food colour.

Variations:

Chocolate butter icing: Add 3-4 teaspoons of sifted cocoa powder to the icing above and beat until the cocoa powder is well mixed into the icing.

Coffee butter icing: Replace vanilla essence with 1 teaspoon of instant coffee powder diluted in ¼ teaspoon water. Beat well.

Mocha butter icing: Add 4 teaspoons of sifted cocoa powder to the coffee butter icing above. Beat well.

Decoration:

Ice the cupcakes and decorate with chocolate buttons, sprinkles, shavings, silver balls, glacé cherries and other candy or fruit.

Banana Cupcakes

Ingredients

Refined flour (maida)	2½ cups
Baking powder	1 tbsp
A pinch of salt	
Unsalted butter	½ cup
Caster sugar	1 cup
Light brown sugar	¾ cup
Eggs	2
Ripe bananas, mashed	4
Buttermilk	2/3 cup
Finely chopped walnuts	½ cup
To decorate	
Honey	½ cup
Banana slices	

Method

- Preheat an oven to 180°C/350°F/Gas 4. Grease and flour 12 cupcake moulds.
- In a small bowl, whisk together the flour, baking powder and salt; set aside.
- In a large bowl, cream the butter, caster sugar and brown sugar together until light and fluffy. Beat in the eggs, one at a time. Mix in the mashed banana.
- Add the flour mixture alternately with the buttermilk to the creamed mixture. Stir in the chopped walnuts.
- Spoon the batter into the prepared cupcake moulds. Bake in the preheated oven for 20 minutes till a skewer inserted comes out clean.
- Remove from the oven, and place on a damp kitchen towel to cool.
- Drizzle some honey over the cupcakes and decorate with sliced bananas tossed in honey.

Chocolate Coffee Cupcakes

Ingredients:

Self-raising flour, sifted	1½ cups
Instant coffee powder	1 tbsp
Dark chocolate, chopped	200 g
Caster sugar	2 cups
Butter	250 g
Hot water	1½ cups
Eggs	2
Vanilla essence	½ tsp
Chocolate icing	
Dark chocolate, chopped	125 g
Unsalted butter	125 g

Method

- Preheat an oven to 180°C/350°F/Gas 4. Grease and flour 12 cupcake moulds.

- Mix together the sifted flour and coffee powder.

- Place the chocolate in a small pan along with the sugar, butter and water and heat gently over a pan of simmering water, until the chocolate and butter melt. Cool and pour into a blender.

- Gradually add the flour-coffee mixture into the blender and blend till well mixed.

- Add the eggs, one at a time, then add the vanilla and blend well.

- Spoon the batter into the prepared moulds and bake in the preheated oven for about 20 minutes, or until a skewer inserted comes out clean. Leave to stand for about 5 minutes.

- For the icing, melt the chocolate and butter in a small pan over a pan of simmering water, and beat with a wooden spoon until smooth. Spread the icing over the cupcakes and mark grooves with a fork for a decorative finish.

DRIED FRUIT KULFI WITH FALOODA

Pankaj Bhadouria

Preparation Time: 10 minutes
Cooking Time: 1 hour 30 minutes + freezing
Serves: 6

Ingredients

Kulfi

Milk	3 litres
Pistachios	4 tbsp
Cashew nuts	4 tbsp
Almonds	4 tbsp
Raisins (*kishmish*)	2 tbsp
Sugar	2 cups

Falooda

Cornflour	2 cups
Saffron (*kesari*) food colour (optional)	½ tsp

To serve

Khus syrup	¾ cup

Tips:

- The dried fruit can be substituted with finely chopped fresh fruit like *chickoo*, strawberries, cherries, mango and oranges. You can also add 250 g thick mango pulp to the cooled milk to make a mango *kulfi*.

- Readymade *falooda* is available easily in summer. Enthusiastic cooks can try out this recipe at home taking care to cook the dough till it attains the required consistency, or you will not be able to press out the *falooda* into noodles.

Method

For the Kulfi

- Pour the milk into a *kadai*. Bring to a boil, reduce heat and simmer, stirring continuously for 20 minutes. Cook till the milk is reduced to around a third (1 litre). Remove from the heat.

- Blanch the nuts in hot water. Drain and peel the almonds. Chop the nuts and raisins. Add sugar and nuts to the warm milk and stir till the sugar is dissolved.

- Pour the mixture into *kulfi* moulds and place in a freezer to set.

For the falooda

- Put the cornflour into a *kadai* with 3 ¾ cups water and the saffron colour and stir until dissolved.

- Cook over medium heat, stirring continuously, until reduced to a gelatinous consistency with a sheen on the surface.

- Force the cooked cornflour through a noodle press into a bowl of ice and chilled water. Store in chilled water in the refrigerator till required.

To serve: Remove the moulds from the freezer. Dip in warm water for 20 seconds and unmould the *kulfi*. Slice in half vertically. Garnish with *falooda* and drizzle with *khus* syrup.

Come summer and the long queues outside the *kulfi* shops speak of the popularity of this Indian ice cream.

At my home, no festival is complete without
a taste of these syrupy morsels.

GULAB JAMUNS WITH RABRI

Pankaj Bhadouria

Preparation Time: 15 minutes + refrigeration
Cooking Time: 90 minutes
Makes: 20 Gulab Jamuns

Rabri

Ingredients

Milk	3 litres
Sugar	350 g
Screw pine (*kewra*) water	½ tsp

Method

- Heat the milk in a *kadai* and bring to a boil. Reduce the heat and stir continuously for 20 minutes. Cook, stirring occasionally, till the milk is reduced to less than a third (around 900 ml) and acquires a granular consistency.

- Remove from the heat and add the sugar. Stir till it dissolves, and add the *kewra* water.

- Leave to cool. Place in a refrigerator to chill for at least 2 hours.

Gulab Jamun

Ingredients

Sugar	900 g
Khoya	500 g
Cottage Cheese (*chhena*)	60 g
Refined flour (*maida*)	4 tbsp
A pinch of soda bicarbonate	
Rose water	1 tsp
Ghee for deep-frying	

Filling

Small *rosogolla*
Dried fruit with *chhena*
Gulkand

Tips: For plain *gulab jamun*, fill with ¼ teaspoon of sugar to ensure they remain soft inside.

Method

- For the filling, chop the ingredients and set aside.

- Cook the sugar with 2½ cups water till it attains a one-string consistency. Keep warm.

- Gently knead the *khoya* to mash any granules. Crumble and mash the *chhena*. Dissolve the soda bicarbonate in 1 teaspoon water.

- Mix together the *khoya*, *chhena*, flour, and soda bicarbonate and knead gently. Divide the mixture into 20 balls. Flatten each ball on your palm and place a little filling on it. Bring the edges of the *khoya* together to enclose the filling completely. Shape into oblongs or balls of different sizes.

- Heat the ghee in a pan. Gently slide in the balls and immediately reduce the heat. Stir the ghee gently with a slotted spoon without touching the balls till they rise to the surface. Cook over low heat until golden brown.

- Remove and immediately immerse in the warm sugar syrup. Leave to soak for 20-25 minutes.

To serve: Drain the warm *gulab jamun* and place in a bowl. Serve with cold *rabri*.

SHRIKHAND TERRINE WITH STRAWBERRY MINT COULIS

Pankaj Bhadouria

Preparation Time: 25 minutes
Cooking Time: 10 minutes
Serves: 4

Shrikhand

Drained (hung) yoghurt*	2 cups
Caster sugar	2½ cups
Vanilla pod OR	1
Vanilla essence	½ tsp

Strawberry Mint Coulis

Strawberries, hulled and roughly chopped	200 g
Mint leaves, roughly torn	½ cup
Sugar	2-3 tbsp
Lemon juice	1 tbsp

To garnish

Mint leaves

*Hang 1kg full fat yoghurt in a piece of muslin or cheesecloth over a bowl in the refrigerator, overnight or for at least 8 hours. Discard the whey.

Tip: If you are making the yoghurt at home you can heat the milk with the vanilla pod or essence to infuse more flavour into the drained yoghurt.

Method

For the shrikhand

*   Whisk the sugar with the drained yoghurt till smooth. Scrape the vanilla pod and remove the seeds. Stir in the seeds or the vanilla essence into the mix.

*   Pour the shrikhand into a terrine mould and place in the freezer to set.

For the strawberry mint coulis

*   Place all the ingredients for the sauce in a pan and cook over a low heat till the sugar melts and the strawberries soften slightly. Do not allow the mixture to get too soft and pulpy. Remove from the heat and set aside to cool.

To serve: Pour the strawberry and mint coulis on a serving platter. Turn out the terrine onto the platter and garnish with mint leaves.

The traditional Marathi dessert is elevated to another plane with the addition of a classic strawberry mint coulis.

Balushahi - another favourite during the festive season.

STUFFED BALUSHAHI

Pankaj Bhadouria

Preparation Time: 40 minutes
Cooking Time: 45 minutes + soaking
Serves: 4

Ingredients

Refined flour (*maida*)	200 g
Soda bicarbonate	½ tsp
Ghee	6 tbsp
Yoghurt, whisked	6 tbsp
Ghee, for frying	3 cups
Sugar	2½ cups
Milk	2 tbsp
Khoya	200 g
Sugar	¼ cup
Mixed dried fruit and nuts	¼ cup

Tips:

- The only fat to be used to make *balushahi* is ghee. Oil is never used for this sweet.

- You can fill the *balushahi* with delicious ingredients such as fresh fruit in a thick syrup or vanilla cream. Let your imagination run wild!

Method

- Sift the flour and soda bicarbonate together into a bowl. Add 6 tablespoons ghee and rub it in with your fingertips till the mixture resembles breadcrumbs.

- Add the whisked yoghurt and knead into a smooth dough. Cover and set the dough aside for 30 minutes.

- Divide the dough into 8 portions and shape into smooth balls. Do not overwork the dough. Make a deep, wide hollow in the centre of each ball with your thumb. Keep the balls covered so they do not dry out.

- Heat the ghee in a *kadai*. Lower the heat and slide in half the *balushahis* and cook in the hot ghee. Make sure that the ghee does not get too hot at any time. If necessary, place a *tawa* under the *kadai*.

- When the *balushahi* float to the top, turn them gently and cook on the other side as well till light golden brown. The whole process will take no less than 30-45 minutes.

- Remove and place on absorbent paper to cool completely.

- For the sugar syrup, place the sugar with 1 cup water in a heavy-bottomed pan, and cook, stirring occasionally, till the sugar dissolves. Bring to a boil and add the milk. Carefully remove the scum that will rise to the surface. Continue to cook till the syrup thickens to a two-string consistency.

- Remove from the heat and add the cooled *balushahi*. Soak them in the syrup for at least 2 hours.

- Carefully remove the *balushahi* from the syrup and set aside on a plate for 2-3 hours till the syrup hardens into a thin white crust.

- For the filling, crumble the *khoya* with your fingers. Place in a pan and cook over a medium heat till soft. Add the sugar and dried fruit and nuts and mix well. Cook, stirring, for 2 minutes, till the sugar dissolves. Remove from heat.

- Spoon the stuffing into the hollows in the *balushahi*.

COFFEE CRÈME BRÛLÉE

Chef Ajay Chopra

Preparation Time: 25 minutes + refrigeration
Cooking Time: 45 minutes
Serves: 6

Ingredients

Cream	2 cups
Granulated sugar	3 tbsp
Espresso coffee OR	2 tbsp
Instant coffee mixed with water	2 tbsp
Egg	1
Egg yolks	3
Demerara sugar	3 tbsp

Method

- Preheat an oven to 120°C/250°F/Gas ½.

- Put the cream, sugar and coffee into a pan and bring to a boil, stirring occasionally.

- Whisk the egg and egg yolks together in a bowl and slowly pour in the hot cream mixture, stirring continuously.

- Pour the mixture into 6 ramekins and place in a roasting tin with water halfway up the sides of the ramekins. Bake in the preheated oven for about 40 minutes till set.

- Remove from the oven and set aside to cool. Place in a refrigerator to chill for at least 2 hours.

To serve: Sprinkle the demerara sugar on top and caramelize with a chef's blowtorch or under a very hot grill. Leave to stand until the top has become crisp, and serve.

Traditional crème brûlée with
a serious caffeine kick!

Elegance and delicate flavours combine to make this dessert a winner!

SAFFRON-POACHED PEARS WITH CINNAMON ICE CREAM

Chef Ajay Chopra

Preparation Time: 45 minutes + refrigeration
Cooking Time: 20-25 minutes
Serves: 4

Poached Pears

Ingredients

Large pears (not too ripe), with stems	4
Caster sugar	175 g
A generous pinch of saffron threads	
Filling	
Thick yoghurt	½ cup
Icing sugar	1 tbsp
Raisins (*kishmish*)	1½ tbsp
Fresh coriander leaves, shredded	10

Method

- Peel the pears, leaving them whole with the stems on. Place in a bowl water to prevent discolouration.
- Put the sugar, 1 litre water and the saffron into a pan in which the pears will just fit in a single layer, and bring slowly to the boil, stirring to dissolve the sugar.
- Add the whole pears, reduce the heat and cook until the pears are tender but still slightly firm.
- Remove from the poaching liquid and leave to cool.
- For the filling, mix together all the ingredients.

Cinnamon Ice Cream

Ingredients

Milk	1 cup
Cream	1 cup
Liquid glucose	4 tbsp
Granulated sugar	3 tbsp
Cinnamon stick	1 large
Large egg yolks	3
Cinnamon powder	1 tsp

Method

- Put the milk, cream, liquid glucose, sugar and cinnamon stick into a pan and bring slowly to the boil, stirring occasionally, till the sugar dissolves. Remove from the heat. Remove the cinnamon stick and discard.
- In a bowl, lightly whisk the egg yolks and cinnamon powder together. Add the milk mixture and mix well. Pour into an ice cream machine and freeze.
- Alternatively, pour into a shallow airtight container and place in the freezer until semi-frozen. Transfer to a chilled bowl and whisk well to break down the ice crystals. Return to the container and place in the freezer again. Repeat this process 3-4 times. Leave until set.

To serve: Using a small scoop, carefully scoop out the pears and spoon in some of the filling. Place each pear on a serving plate and drizzle over a little poaching liquid. Serve with scoops of cinnamon ice cream.

COINTREAU-SOAKED MALPUA
WITH WHIPPED CREAM

Chef Kunal Kapoor

Preparation Time: 30 minutes
Cooking Time: 15 minutes
Serves: 4

Ingredients

Sugar	250 g
Cointreau (orange liqueur)	200 ml
A pinch of saffron	
Milk	½ cup
Khoya	100 g
Refined flour (*maida*)	150 g
Fennel seeds (*badi saunf*)	1 tsp
Vegetable oil for frying	1 cup
Grated rind of 2 large oranges	
Whipped cream, sweetened	200 g
Garnish	
Pistachio slivers	20 g

Method

- For the sugar syrup, in a pan mix the sugar with 1 cup water and cook till reduced to half its original volume. Remove from heat and leave to cool. Stir in 150 ml Cointreau.

- In a bowl, soak the saffron in 1 tablespoon warm water.

- Combine the milk and 3 tablespoons water.

- In a heavy bowl, mash the *khoya* with the palm of your hand. Gradually add the flour and milk and keep mixing. Once it reaches a thick pouring consistency, add the fennel and saffron.

- Heat the oil in a frying pan. Pour a ladleful of the batter into the pan and spread with the back of the ladle to make a thick round pancake. Fry till light golden brown. Remove and dip in the Cointreau-flavoured syrup.

- In a bowl, mix together the orange rind and remaining Cointreau. Gently fold in the whipped cream.

To serve: Place the hot *malpuas* on a plate. Top with a dollop of whipped Cointreau-flavoured cream and sprinkle with pistachios.

128

Cointreau gives this traditional Indian dessert a delightful French twist.

DOUBLE KA MEETHA

Sliced Bread Pudding

Chef Kunal Kapoor

Preparation Time: 10 minutes
Cooking Time: 30 minutes
Serves: 4

Ingredients

Full cream milk	1½ litres
Fennel (*badi saunf*)	1 tbsp
Sugar	400 g
A pinch of saffron	
Khoya	150 g
Green cardamom powder	2 tsp
Screw pine (*kewra*) water	2 tsp
Rose water	2 tsp
Thick slices of milk bread	8
Oil	300 ml

To garnish

Pistachio slivers	50 g
Almond slivers	50 g

Method

- Heat the milk in a heavy-bottomed pan; add the fennel, sugar, saffron, *khoya*, cardamom powder, *kewra* and rose waters. Bring to a boil and remove from the heat.

- Trim the crust off the bread slices.

- In a large shallow frying pan, gently heat the oil. Add the bread slices and on a low heat shallow-fry them on both sides, turning frequently. Take care not to break or burn them.

- Increase the heat and slowly pour the flavoured milk into the pan. Be careful you do not get scalded by the steam produced.

- Lower the heat and cook till all the milk is absorbed by the bread. Remove from the heat and cool slightly. Place the pan in a refrigerator to chill.

To serve: Arrange the slices on a plate and garnish with pistachio and almond slivers.

From Nizami kitchens to your table – opulence on a plate!

MasterChef
Kitchen

MasterChef Pankaj's Grand Finale dish impressed the entire nation and won her the coveted title of India's first MasterChef, prompting Akshay Kumar to proclaim, "Pankaj has magic in her hands!"

DRUNKEN CHICKEN LOG

Pankaj Bhadouria

Preparation Time: 45 minutes
Cooking Time: 25 minutes
Serves: 4

Ingredients

Boneless, skinless chicken breasts	3
Dry red wine	1 cup
Salt to taste	
Long grain rice (*basmati*)	1 cup
Fresh button mushrooms, finely chopped	100 g
Fresh thyme, finely chopped	4 sprigs
Pitted black olives, sliced	¼ cup
Gouda cheese, grated	100 g
Processed cheese, grated	150 g
Black pepper powder	1 tsp
Olive oil	3 tbsp
Honey	2 tbsp
Brandy	4 tsp
Butter, chilled	20 g

To serve

Lettuce leaves

Method

- Split each chicken breast in half, slicing through without separating the halves. Open out like a sheet. Flatten with a meat hammer or rolling pin between 2 sheets of cling film to make a rectangle.

- Marinate the chicken in 2½ tablespoons red wine and salt in a bowl for 15 minutes.

- In a large pan, boil the rice with salt and 4 cups water and drain when done.

- Add the mushrooms, half the thyme, the olives, both cheeses, salt and pepper to the rice. Mix well and divide into three parts. Shape each part into a log.

- Place a rice log at one end of each flattened chicken breast and carefully roll it up ensuring that the rice log is completely covered and one end of the chicken overlaps the other. Secure the roll with a thread and refrigerate for 15-20 minutes.

- Heat the olive oil in a pan; add the chicken logs and brown on all sides.

- Add the remaining red wine and remaining thyme and cook till the chicken is almost done. Add the honey and cook till done. Remove the chicken from the pan.

- Heat the brandy in a ladle till bubbles begin to appear around the edges. Add to the hot pan to flambé (flame) the sauce. Reduce the sauce to approximately 2½ tablespoons. Remove the pan from the heat and add the cold butter and stir well.

To serve: Slice the chicken log and arrange the slices on a platter lined with lettuce leaves. Drizzle the wine sauce over and around the slices.

AUBERGINE ROLLS WITH OLIVE TAPENADE AND GARLIC YOGHURT CHEESE

Kandla Nijhowne

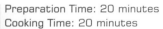

Preparation Time: 20 minutes
Cooking Time: 20 minutes
Serves: 4

Ingredients

Slim, long purple aubergines (brinjals)	8-9
Salt	½ tsp
Aubergines (brinjals)	2 small
Yoghurt, drained (hung)	1½ kg
Cherry tomatoes, quartered	20-25
A few sprigs of basil, shredded	
A piece of coal	
Ghee	1 tsp

Tapenade

Pimento-stuffed olives, finely chopped	20-25
Capers, finely chopped	2-3 tbsp
Olive oil	1¼ cups
Garlic, finely chopped	8 large cloves
Parmesan cheese, grated	150 g
Black pepper powder	½ tsp

Method

- Slice the long aubergines lengthways into thin strips. Sprinkle with salt and set aside.

- Brush the 2 small whole aubergines with oil and roast over an open gas flame. Keep turning to avoid burning. Peel and mash with a fork.

- For the tapenade, combine the olives, capers, 4 tablespoons olive oil, pepper, half the garlic and parmesan cheese. Set aside.

- Rinse and pat the aubergine strips dry, and toss in 1 tablespoon olive oil. Heat a griddle and grill the strips on both sides.

- Heat the piece of coal till it is red hot. Arrange the grilled aubergine strips on a plate. Place the hot coal in a small bowl and place on the plate with the aubergines. Pour ghee over the coal and immediately cover the plate with a deep lid. Let the aubergines absorb the smoky flavour for a few seconds.

- For the yoghurt cheese, in a bowl, mix the mashed roasted aubergines with the drained yoghurt, half the remaining garlic, salt and pepper and refrigerate till chilled.

- Arrange the smoked aubergine strips side by side and spread a little tapenade on each one. Roll up each strip and fasten with a toothpick.

- Heat 2 tablespoons olive oil, add the remaining garlic and sauté till golden. Toss in cherry tomatoes, basil, salt and pepper.

To serve: Place mounds of yoghurt cheese on a plate and place the aubergine rolls on top. Drizzle with the garlic and basil-infused oil and cherry tomato mixture.

Kandla turned out this Mediterranean-style dish for the Reunion episode and it became an instant hit with the contestants' families.

This is Smita's heirloom recipe which won her and Kandla high praise from HRH Sriji Arvind Singh Mewar. Being a Rajasthani herself, she deemed it a great honour to cook for the Maharana.

BADAMI SUBZ FATEHPURI

Vegetables and Gram Flour Dumplings
in a Creamy Almond Gravy

Smita Dugar and Kandla Nijhowne

Preparation Time: 30 minutes
Cooking Time: 35 minutes
Serves: 4-6

Ingredients

Cauliflower florets	100 g
Carrot, cut into cubes	1 large
French beans, cut into 1-inch pieces	50 g
Ghee	3 tbsp
Green cardamoms	2

Method

- Blanch the cauliflower, carrots and French beans in boiling water. Drain, refresh in cold water and drain again. Set aside.

- Heat 1 tablespoon ghee in a pan; add the cardamoms, peppercorns, cinnamon and cloves, and fry till fragrant and remove.

Black peppercorns	2-3
Cinnamon	1-inch stick
Cloves	2-3
Garlic paste	1 tsp
Boiled onion paste	2 tbsp
Tomato purée	3 tbsp
Browned onion paste	1 tbsp
Turmeric powder	½ tbsp
Red chilli powder	1 tbsp
Coriander powder	1 tsp
Cumin seeds	½ tsp
Coriander seeds	½ tsp
Finely chopped ginger	1 tsp
Finely chopped green chilli	1 tsp
Almond paste	1 tbsp
Cream	2 tbsp
Gatte (recipe below)	100 g
Sugar	½ tsp
Salt to taste	
Finely chopped coriander	2 tbsp

- Add the garlic paste and boiled onion paste to the pan and sauté for a few minutes. Add the tomato purée and browned onion paste, and sauté till the ghee separates.

- Mix in the turmeric, chilli and coriander powders. Crush the fried whole spices and add to the pan; sauté till the ghee separates. Add 1 cup water, stir and bring to a boil.

- Remove from the heat and strain the mixture. Return the strained gravy to the pan and purée the residue in a blender. Strain again and add to the pan with a little water if necessary.

- Heat the remaining ghee in another pan; add the cumin seeds and coriander seeds and sauté till well browned and fragrant. Add the ginger, green chilli and the gravy.

- Stir in the almond paste, blanched vegetables, *gatte*, sugar and salt. Bring to a boil and stir in the cream. Sprinkle with fresh coriander and serve hot.

Gatte

Ingredients

Gram flour (*besan*)	100 g
A pinch of asafoetida (*hing*)	
Red chilli powder	½ tsp
Coriander powder	1 tsp
Dried fenugreek leaves (*kasoori methi*)	1 tsp
Salt to taste	
Turmeric powder	¼ tsp
Oil for deep-frying	

Method

- Combine all the ingredients except the oil. Shape into small lemon-sized balls.

- Bring a pan of water to a boil, add the *gatte* and cook till tender. Drain, pat dry and set aside.

- Heat the oil in a *kadai* and deep-fry the *gatte* till golden. Remove and drain on absorbent paper.

To serve: Transfer the vegetables to a bowl. Serve with *roti* and pickles on the side.

CHETTINAD-STYLE FISH WITH COCONUT RICE AND CURRIED COCONUT SAUCE

Chef Ajay's Blue Team

Preparation Time: 15 minutes
Cooking Time: 45 minutes
Serves: 4

Chettinad Fish

Ingredients

Indian salmon (*rawas*) fillets	8
Salt	¼ tsp
Lemon juice	2 tbsp
Oil	1 tbsp
Chettinad Masala	
Oil	1 tsp
Dried red chillies	4-5
Cloves	2
Mace (*javitri*)	4 blades
Green cardamoms	2
Bay leaves	2
Cumin seeds	1 tsp
Fennel seeds (*badi saunf*)	1 tsp
Fenugreek seeds (*methi dana*)	½ tsp
Coriander seeds	2 tsp
Black peppercorns	8-12

Method

- Marinate the fish in salt and lemon juice for 15-20 minutes.
- For the Chettinad *masala*, heat the oil in a pan and lightly sauté the dried chillies, cloves, mace, cardamoms, bay leaves, cumin seeds, fennel seeds, fenugreek seeds, coriander seeds and black peppercorns. Cool and grind to a fine powder.
- Coat the flesh side of the fish with the prepared Chettinad *masala* and set aside for 20 minutes.
- Heat the oil in a frying pan and shallow-fry the *rawas*, skin side down, till golden brown. Turn the fillets over and cook the other side.

Coconut Rice

Ingredients

Basmati rice	200 g
Salt	½ tsp
Coconut oil	2 tbsp
Mustard seeds	1 tsp
Curry leaves	8-10
Split Bengal gram (*chana dal*)	1 tsp
Split black gram (*urad dal*)	1 tsp
Finely chopped green chillies	1 tbsp
Ginger, finely chopped	1½ inches
Desiccated coconut	3 tbsp
Finely chopped coriander	3 tbsp

Method

- In a large pan, boil the rice with salt and 5 cups water till tender. Drain.
- Heat the coconut oil in a *kadai* and add the mustard seeds. When the seeds begin to splutter, add the curry leaves, and both *dals* and fry till the *dals* turn golden brown.
- Add the chillies, ginger and coconut and sauté for 2 minutes. Add the rice and chopped coriander, and toss gently to mix.

Curried Coconut Sauce

Ingredients

Coconut oil	2 tbsp
Mustard seeds	1 tsp
Curry leaves	9-10
Split black gram (*urad dal*)	1 tsp
Split Bengal gram (*chana dal*)	1 tsp
Dried red chillies	3-4
Turmeric powder	¼ tsp
Finely sliced onion	2 tsp
Finely sliced tomato	1 tbsp
Fish stock or water	½ cup
Coconut milk	1 cup
Lemon juice	2 tsp
Salt	¼ tsp

Method

- Heat the coconut oil in a *kadai* and add the mustard seeds. When the seeds begin to splutter, add the curry leaves and both *dals* and fry till the *dals* are golden brown.

- Add the red chillies, turmeric and onion and sauté till the onions turn golden. Add the tomato, fish stock or water and bring to a boil, stirring continuously.

- Add the coconut milk, lower the heat and simmer till slightly thick. Stir in the lemon juice and salt.

To serve: Place the *rawas* fillets on a platter. Pack the coconut rice into a small mould and turn out onto the plate. Drizzle coconut curry over the rice.

This dish was created by Chef Ajay's Blue team for Bollywood stars Randhir and Rishi Kapoor, who were extravagant in their praise.

SPINACH AND DILL CANNELLONI WITH TULSI MAKHANI SAUCE

Chef Kunal's Red Team

Preparation Time: 15 minutes
Cooking Time: 40 minutes
Serves: 4

Ingredients

Cannelloni

Cottage cheese	250 g
Cornflour	2 tbsp
Salt to taste	
Butter	1 tbsp
Finely chopped garlic	1 tsp
Onion, finely chopped	1 medium
Spinach, blanched and finely chopped	200 g
Black pepper powder	½ tsp
Finely chopped dill	2 tbsp
Semolina	2 tbsp
Vegetable oil for deep-frying	

Tulsi makhani sauce

Tomatoes, diced	12
Onion, diced	1
Garlic	5 cloves
Ginger	½ inch
Cashew nuts	1 tbsp
Black peppercorns	4
Green cardamom	1
Fresh basil	2 sprigs
Dried fenugreek leaves (kasoori methi)	½ tsp
Butter	2 tbsp
Cream	1 tbsp

To garnish

Fresh coriander leaves

Method

For the cannelloni

- Mash the cottage cheese and combine with the cornflour and salt. Divide the mixture into 4 portions.

- Heat the butter in a pan; add the garlic and onion and sauté till the onion is translucent. Mix in the spinach, salt and pepper and cook for 2 more minutes. Remove from heat and stir in the dill.

- Flatten a portion of cheese mixture on your palm. Spoon a quarter of the spinach mixture on it and roll up to form a cylinder. Seal the sides. Make 4 cylinders.

- Heat the oil in a kadai. Roll the cylinders in semolina and deep-fry till golden. Remove and drain on absorbent paper.

For the makhani sauce

- Boil 3 cups water in a deep saucepan and put in all the ingredients except the kasoori methi, butter and cream. Cook till the tomatoes are soft and pulpy. Purée the mixture in a blender and strain.

- Heat a kadai and add the butter. When the butter melts, add the puréed tomato mixture and salt and cook for 12 minutes. Check the seasoning.

- Stir in the kasoori methi and cream.

To serve: Pour some of the gravy into a bowl. Cut the cannelloni crosswise and place in the gravy. Garnish with fresh coriander.

This recipe was created by the Red Team under the mentorship of Chef Kunal for the MasterChef Bollywood Special episode. It was greeted by exclamations of delight from Rishi and Randhir Kapoor.

This was MasterChef runner-up Jayanandan's Grand Finale dish, which Farah Khan said was testimony to his great passion for food.

CRISP CHICKEN 'N' CHEESE BASKET WITH BURNT GARLIC SAUCE

Jayanandan Bhaskar

Preparation Time: 15 minutes
Cooking Time: 40 minutes + baking
Serves: 4

Chicken 'n' Cheese Basket

Ingredients

Gouda cheese, cut into short fingers	100 g
Green peppercorns, crushed	1 tbsp
Finely chopped black olives	1 tbsp
Finely chopped green olives	1 tbsp
Jalapeño chillies, finely chopped	2
White vinegar	1 tsp
Olive oil	1 tsp

Method

- In a bowl, marinate the cheese fingers in a mixture of crushed green peppercorns, olives, jalapeños, vinegar, olive oil, salt and pepper for 10 minutes.

- Heat the butter in a pan; add the garlic, green chillies and onion and sauté till the onion turns golden. Mix in the thyme, parsley, rosemary and minced chicken. Cook, stirring, for 2-3 minutes on a low heat.

Salt to taste

Black pepper powder to taste

Butter	2 tbsp
Garlic, finely chopped	3-4 cloves
Green chillies, finely chopped	2
Onion, finely chopped	1 medium
Dried thyme	1 tsp
Dried parsley	1 tsp
Dried rosemary, crushed	1 tsp
Minced chicken	500 g
Red chilli flakes	1 tsp
Dried oregano	½ tsp
Worcestershire sauce	1 tsp
Wonton sheets, cut into 1-inch wide strips	6
Eggs, beaten	2

- Add the chilli flakes, oregano, black pepper and Worcestershire sauce, and cook till the chicken is tender.

- On a dry chopping board, arrange 8 wonton strips side by side and weave 8 more horizontal wonton strips into them. The final product should look like a woven mat. Repeat the process with remaining strips to make 4 mats.

- Preheat an oven to 180°C/350°F/Gas 4. Grease a baking tray.

- Brush the prepared 'mats' with the beaten egg and carefully place egg side up in a small strainer. Fill with the cheese mixture and top with the chicken mince. Fold in the ends of the mat, so they overlap each other. Brush with egg wash to seal well.

- Invert the filled wonton baskets onto a greased baking tray and brush with more egg wash. Bake in the preheated oven till the wonton strips are golden and crisp.

Burnt Garlic Cream Sauce

Ingredients

Butter	1½ tbsp
Garlic, finely chopped	2-3 cloves
White wine	2 tbsp
Fresh cream	4 tbsp
Salt to taste	
Black pepper powder	1 tsp

Method

- Heat the butter in a pan; add the garlic and sauté on a high heat till brown.

- Add the wine and cook for 10 to 15 seconds. Remove the pan from the heat and stir in the cream, salt and pepper. Mix well.

To serve: Arrange the hot chicken baskets on a platter. Serve with the burnt garlic sauce.

LAZZAT - E - NIWALA

Mushroom and Cottage Cheese Kebabs with Green Coriander and Smoked Yoghurt Dips

Chef Kunal's Red Team

Preparation Time: 15 minutes
Cooking Time: 25-30 minutes
Serves: 12-16 kebabs

Mushroom and Cottage Cheese Kebabs

Ingredients

Butter	½ tbsp
Diced onion	1 tbsp
Fresh button mushrooms, diced	100 g
Ginger-garlic paste	1 tsp
Salt	½ tsp
Finely chopped green chilli	1 tsp
Coriander leaves, finely chopped	1 tbsp
Paneer, mashed	200 g
Red chilli powder	1 tsp
Split Bengal gram (*chana dal*), roasted and coarsely ground	½ cup
Black pepper powder	1 tsp
Cumin powder	1 tsp
Cinnamon powder	1 tsp
Dried breadcrumbs	1 cup
Ghee or oil for shallow-frying	

Method

- Heat the butter in a pan; add the onion and sauté till translucent. Add the mushrooms, ginger-garlic paste, salt, green chilli and coriander leaves; saute on a high heat till the water evaporates.

- Combine the *paneer* with the chilli powder, ground *chana dal*, pepper, cumin powder and cinnamon powder and mix well. Divide the mixture into 12-16 parts.

- Flatten each part on your palm and fill with the mushroom mixture. Gather the edges together to enclose the filling and shape into a kebab. Roll the kebab in breadcrumbs.

- Heat the ghee in a frying pan and shallow-fry the kebabs till golden brown on both sides. Remove and drain on absorbent paper.

Green Coriander Dip

Ingredients

Coriander leaves	1 cup
Green chillies, chopped	3
Mint leaves	½ cup
Finely chopped onion	1 tbsp
Finely chopped garlic	1 tsp
Salt	½ tsp
Lemon juice	2 tsp

Method

- Place the coriander, green chillies, mint, onion, garlic, salt and lemon juice in a blender and blend to a smooth paste. Place in a refrigerator to chill.

Smoked Yoghurt Dip

Ingredients

Drained (hung) yoghurt	50 g
Cumin powder, roasted	1 tsp
Grated cucumber	2 tbsp
Red chilli powder	1 tsp
Salt to taste	
A piece of charcoal	

Method

- Combine the drained yoghurt with the cumin powder, cucumber, chilli powder and salt. Transfer to a small bowl and place on a plate.

- Heat the coal on an open flame till red hot and place in another small bowl. Place the bowl next to the one containing the yoghurt dip.

- Drizzle a few drops of butter on the coal and immediately cover both bowls with a large inverted pan or *handi*. Let the dip absorb the smoky flavour of the coal for a few seconds. Remove, cover the bowl with cling film and place in a refrigerator to chill.

To serve: Arrange the kebabs in a serving dish. Transfer the dips into bowls and serve with the kebabs.

This dish was conceptualised by the Red Team and was commended by all 3 judges for its simplicity and blend of flavours.

Chef Ajay's signature dish amazed the scions of the first family of Bollywood - Randhir and Rishi Kapoor, who were awestruck by the transformation of this simple Rajasthani dish into a perfect example of modern Indian cuisine.

PITHORE, MATAR MASALA AUR TAMATAR KI KADHI

Fried Gram Flour Cakes with Curried Green Peas and
Tomato Yoghurt Sauce

Chef Ajay's Blue Team

Preparation Time: 1 hour
Cooking Time: 45 minutes
Serves: 6-8

Pithore

Ingredients

Yoghurt, drained (hung)	1 ½ kg
Gram flour (*besan*)	500 g
Red chilli powder	1 tbsp
Turmeric powder	1 tbsp
Salt	½ tsp
Semolina (*sooji*)	4 tbsp
Ghee	4 tbsp
Khada masala	
Coriander seeds	2 tbsp
Fennel seeds (*badi saunf*)	½ tbsp
Cumin seeds	½ tbsp
Black peppercorns	½ tbsp
Dried red chillies	2-3

Method

- In a bowl, combine the drained yoghurt with the gram flour, chilli powder, turmeric powder and salt. Set aside.

- For the *khada masala*, in a pan, separately roast the coriander seeds, fennel seeds, cumin seeds, peppercorns and dried red chillies. Combine and grind to a fine powder. Combine the ground spices with the yoghurt mixture.

- Heat 3 tablespoons ghee in a large frying pan; add the yoghurt mixture and cook, stirring continuously, for 10-15 minutes till very thick.

- Remove from heat and pour into a greased tray and freeze for half an hour till firmly set. Cut into round cakes (*pithore*) with a ring cutter. Roll the cakes in the semolina.

- Heat 1 tablespoon ghee on a *tawa* and shallow-fry the *pithore* on both sides till golden.

Matar Masala

Ingredients

Vegetable oil	1 tbsp
Garlic, finely chopped	6-8 cloves
Ginger, finely chopped	1 inch
Onions, finely chopped	2
Tomatoes, finely chopped	2
Turmeric powder	1 tsp
Red chilli powder	1 tsp
Garam masala powder	1 tsp
Cumin powder	½ tsp
Coriander powder	½ tsp
Fresh shelled green peas, parboiled	350 g
Salt	½ tsp

Method

- In a pan, heat the oil; add the garlic and ginger and sauté for a few seconds.
- Mix in the onions, tomatoes and all the spices and cook till the oil separates from the mixture.
- Add the green peas and salt and cook till the peas are tender.

Tamatar ki Kadhi

Ingredients

Yogurt	1 ½ cups
Ginger-garlic paste	2 tbsp
Salt	1 tsp
Coriander powder	1 tsp
Turmeric powder	1 tsp
Ghee	3 tbsp
Mustard seeds	½ tsp
Curry leaves	10-12
Dried red chillies	2
A pinch of asafoetida (*hing*)	
Tomato purée	5 tbsp

Method

- In a bowl, mix together the yoghurt, 1 tablespoon ginger-garlic paste, salt, coriander powder and turmeric powder.
- Heat the ghee in a thick-bottomed pan; add the mustard seeds, curry leaves and whole red chillies and sauté till the spices begin to splutter.
- Add the remaining ginger-garlic paste and sauté for 3-4 minutes.
- Add the asafoetida and mix well. Add the tomato purée and sauté for a few minutes till the ghee separates.
- Add the yoghurt mixture and bring to a boil, stirring continuously. Lower the heat and simmer for about 25 minutes.
- Strain the *kadhi* and keep hot.

Mathri

Ingredients

Refined flour (*maida*)	1 cup
Carom seeds (*ajwain*)	½ tsp
Salt	½ tsp
Vegetable oil for deep-frying	

Method

- Combine the flour, carom seeds, salt and 1 tablespoon hot oil. Add water and knead to make a smooth stiff dough.

- Divide the dough into small portions and roll out each portion into a rectangle. Cut into triangles.

- Heat the oil in a *kadai*. Deep-fry the triangles (*mathri*) till golden and crisp. Remove and drain on absorbent paper.

To serve: Spoon some *matar masala* into the centre of a plate, place a *pithore* cake on top and place a *mathri* over it. Repeat the layers. Drizzle tomato *kadhi* around.

Kandla and Smita won accolades for this dish from Sriji HRH Arvind Singh Mewar, who deemed it worthy to be on the royal menu.

LEHRIYA MIRCH AUR PISTA PUDINA CHUTNEY

Crisp Pastry-covered Stuffed Chillies with Minty
Pistachio Chutney

Kandla Nijhowne and Smita Dugar

Preparation Time: 30 minutes
Cooking Time: 20 minutes + baking
Serves: 4

Lehriya Mirch

Ingredients

Large Jodhpuri green chillies	4
Egg, beaten	1
Vegetable oil	1¼ cups
Stuffing	
Ghee	4 tbsp
Onion, minced	1 large
Ginger, chopped	½ inch
Green chilli, finely chopped	1
Minced mutton	250 g
Cashew nuts, roasted and chopped	4-5
Shelled green peas, boiled	100 g
Salt	½ tsp
Black pepper powder	½ tsp
Pastry	
Refined flour (*maida*)	100 g
Oil	2 tbsp
Salt	½ tsp
Carom seeds (*ajwain*)	1 tsp

Method

- Wash and slit the chillies to make a pocket. Remove the seeds.

- For the stuffing, heat the ghee in a pan and fry the onion till brown. Add the chopped ginger and green chilli and cook for a few seconds.

- Add the minced mutton and brown thoroughly, stirring continuously to prevent sticking. Remove from heat and set aside to cool. Break up any lumps.

- Add the roasted cashew nuts, boiled peas, salt and pepper and mix well. Stuff the mixture into the slit chillies.

- For the pastry, combine the flour, oil, salt and *ajwain* with water to make a stiff dough. Roll out the dough and cut into ¾-inch wide strips with a pizza cutter.

- Starting at one end, carefully wrap the strips of dough around the chillies, sealing as you go along with beaten egg.

- Heat the oil in a *kadai* and deep-fry the pastry-covered chillies till crisp and golden brown. Drain on absorbent paper.

Pista Pudina Chutney

Ingredients

Mint leaves	1 cup
Garlic	3-4 cloves
Green chillies	2
Ginger	½ inch
Pistachios, soaked	¼ cup
Juice of ½ lemon	
Salt	¼ tsp

Method

- Grind together the mint, garlic, chillies, ginger and pistachios, reserving a few pistachios for garnishing.

- Add the lemon juice and salt and mix well.

- Cut the reserved pistachios into thin slivers and sprinkle over the chutney.

SWEET 'N' SOUR LAMB CHOPS WITH MASHED POTATO AND STIR-FRIED PESTO VEGETABLES

Joe Baath

Preparation Time: 30 minutes + marination
Cooking Time: 45 minutes
Serves: 4

Lamb Chops

Ingredients

Orange juice	1½ cups
Pineapple juice	1½ cups
Onions, finely chopped	2 medium
Garlic, finely chopped	15-20 cloves
Fresh rosemary, finely chopped	2 tsp
OR dried rosemary, crushed	1 tsp
Salt to taste	
Lamb chops	8
Olive oil	1 tbsp
Chilled butter	1 tbsp

Method

- Mix together the orange juice, pineapple juice, onions, garlic, rosemary and salt. Marinate the lamb chops in the mixture, preferably in a refrigerator, for 2 hours.

- Heat the olive oil in a heavy-bottomed frying pan and sear the lamb chops on both sides until tender and caramelised. Remove the lamb chops.

- Cook the juices left in the pan till thick and add the chilled butter. Stir till melted and smooth to make a glaze.

Mashed Potato

Ingredients

Potatoes, boiled in salted water	6 medium
Butter	3 tbsp
Milk	¾ cup
Finely chopped garlic	1 tbsp
Finely chopped fresh parsley	½ tbsp
Dried oregano	1 tsp
Salt to taste	
Black pepper powder	½ tsp

Method

- Peel and mash the potatoes till smooth. Add the butter and milk and mix well. Cook on a low heat, stirring continuously.

- Add the garlic, parsley, oregano, salt and pepper and mix well. Cook for 2 more minutes and set aside.

Pesto Vegetables

Ingredients

Basil leaves	2 tbsp
Grated parmesan cheese	⅓ cup
Garlic	6-8 cloves
Pine nuts (*chilgoza*)	⅓ cup
Olive oil	⅓ cup
Butter	2 tbsp
Diagonally sliced baby corn	½ cup
Quartered button mushrooms	½ cup
Broccoli florets	½ cup
Cauliflower florets	⅓ cup
Green zucchini, diced	1
Yellow zucchini, diced	1
Red capsicums, diced	2
Salt to taste	

Method

- Blend the basil, parmesan cheese, half the garlic, the pine nuts and olive oil in a blender to a fine paste. Set aside.

- Heat the butter in a wok. Add the garlic, baby corn, mushrooms and broccoli and sauté on a high heat for a few seconds.

- Add the cauliflower and zucchini and sauté for a few minutes. Add the capsicums, toss to mix, and add the pesto. Toss on a high heat for a few seconds.

To serve: Arrange the lamb chops on a bed of mashed potato and drizzle with the glaze. Arrange the pesto vegetables on the side.

This dish created by Joe Baath was one of the most highly-commended dishes in the MasterChef Kitchen.

Pritesh had never cooked with *khoya* before, but for the MasterChef Diwali task, he created a fabulous dessert with the given ingredients and became the top contestant of the week.

CREAMY, CRUNCHY ORANGE SURPRISE

Pritesh Chothani

Preparation Time: 20 minutes
Cooking Time: 30 minutes
Serves: 4-6

Ingredients

Refined flour (*maida*)	200 g
Semolina (*sooji*)	50 g
Ghee	2 tbsp
A pinch of salt	
Oil	1 cup
Zest and juice of 2 oranges	
Khoya, grated	100 g
Cottage cheese (*paneer*), grated	100 g
Dried rose petals	⅓ cup
Powdered sugar	100 g
Dried fruit	1 tbsp

Method

- Combine the flour, semolina, ghee and salt. Knead with a little water to make a stiff dough. Wrap in cling film and set aside for 15 minutes.

- Heat the oil in a *kadai*. Divide the dough into 12 small balls. Roll out each ball thinly and press over the outside of a tart mould to give it a '*katori*' shape. Gently place it in the hot oil and deep-fry on a low heat. Remove and drain on absorbent paper.

- Heat the orange juice in a pan and cook till thick and syrupy.

- In another pan, cook the *khoya* till soft, moist and slightly golden. Mix in the *paneer* and mash together to form a thick smooth paste.

- Combine the rose petals with half a cup of water and powdered sugar in a separate pan, and cook till thick and syrupy. Add to the *khoya-paneer* mixture and mix well. Add the reduced orange juice and mix well. Cool slightly.

To serve: Fill a piping bag with the *khoya-paneer* mixture and pipe it into the prepared *katori*. Arrange on a serving plate and garnish with dried fruit and orange zest.

RASGULLA CAKE

MasterChef Kitchen

Preparation Time: 60 minutes
Cooking Time: 30 minutes
Serves: 10-12 generous portions

Ingredients

Eggless chocolate sponge

Refined flour (*maida*)	200 g
Baking powder	1 tsp
Soda bicarbonate	¾ tbsp
Cocoa powder	6 tbsp
Milk	5 tbsp
Yoghurt	1 cup
Caster sugar	100 g
White butter	100 g
Vanilla essence	¼ tsp

Rasgulla

Cottage cheese (*chhena*)	500 g
Star anise (*chakri phool*)	2
Sugar	1 cup

Fillings

Non-dairy cream, whipped	2 cups
Tangerines, segmented	3
Sweet limes (*mosambi*), segmented	3
Melon	1 large
Chocolate	200 g

Method

For the chocolate sponge

- Preheat an oven to 170°C/325°F/Gas 3. Grease a 6-inch round cake tin and line it with greaseproof paper.

- Sift the flour, baking powder, soda bicarbonate and cocoa powder together. Heat the milk till it is lukewarm.

- Whisk the yoghurt, caster sugar, butter and vanilla essence together till smooth and frothy.

- Fold in the flour mixture alternately with the milk. Mix quickly, but gently, to a smooth batter.

- Pour the batter into the prepared cake tin and bake in the preheated oven on the centre rack for 30 minutes.

- Check if the cake is done by inserting a skewer or knife into the centre. If it comes out clean, remove the cake from the oven and after a few seconds, turn it out onto a wire rack and leave to cool.

For the rasgulla

- In a saucepan, mix 2 cups of sugar with half a cup of water and the star anise. Place on heat and stir till the sugar dissolves. Bring the mixture to a boil. Clarify the syrup by spooning off the grey layer or scum that has risen to the top.

- While the sugar syrup is cooking, grate or crumble the *chhena*. Knead till very smooth and light. Shape into small balls.

- Gently add the *chhena* balls to the boiling sugar syrup and poach them till soft.

- To test whether *rasgulla* are cooked, drop one into a deep bowl of water. If it sinks to the bottom, the *rasgulla* is cooked.

- Remove the *rasgulla* from the syrup with a slotted spoon and set aside.

To assemble the cake

- Cut the cake into two horizontal layers. Cut *rasgulla* in half. Place one layer of the cake on a presentation plate. Arrange the *rasgulla* and half the tangerine and sweet lime segments on top. Cover with the second layer of sponge.

- Spread a layer of cream on the top and sides.

- Pipe the remaining cream with a star-shaped nozzle on top of the cake.

- Scoop out the melon using a melon baller. Place some melon balls on top of the piped cream.

- Place the cake in the refrigerator to chill and set.

- Melt chocolate and spread over a metal sheet that has been covered with cling wrap. Refrigerate. When the chocolate has set, break off pieces and use to decorate the cake on the top and sides.

To serve: Cut the cake in wedges and serve.

For one of the most-difficult Pressure Tasks of MasterChef Kitchen, Radhicka made the finest Rasgulla Cake among all the contestants. Her cake was presented to the Bachchan *bahu*, Aishwarya, who presented Radhicka with a personalised gift for introducing her to the 'fantastic and wonderful' cake.

This exotic *seviyan* dessert by Zebi brought tears to Akshay Kumar's eyes, and like a baby he refused to part with the bowl!

BENARSI KEMAMI SEVIYAN

Benares-style Vermicelli in a Rich Aromatic Dried Fruit Sauce

Zebi Zubair

Preparation Time: 30 minutes
Cooking Time: 1 hour
Serves: 12

Ingredients

Sugar	½ kg
Khoya	½ kg
Milk	2½ cups
Water	2½ cups
Very fine vermicelli (Benarsi *seviyan*)	½ kg
Pure ghee	250 g
Fox nuts (*makhana*), chopped	25 g
Cashew nuts	50 g
Almonds	50 g
Raisins (*kishmish*)	50 g
Chopped dried coconut (*gari*)	½ cup
Screw pine (*kewra*) essence	3 drops
Green cardamoms	10
Nutmeg, grated	½
Edible silver foil (*chandi ka varq*)	5 pieces

Method

- In a pan, mix together the sugar, *khoya*, milk and water. Place the pan on heat and cook till the mixture thickens and attains a 3-4 string consistency (3-4 *taar ki chashni*), or till the mixture starts to turn brown and bubble.

- In another pan, roast the *seviyan* till dark brown. Remove and set aside.

- In the same pan, heat the ghee and fry the chopped *makhana* and remove. Fry the chopped coconut and other dried fruit in the ghee one by one, separately.

- Add the roasted *seviyan* to the *chashni* and mix well. Add all the fried ingredients and stir. Cook for 2 minutes and remove from heat. Cover the pan and leave to stand for at least 10 minutes. Add the *kewra* essence and sprinkle the nutmeg and green cardamom powder.

To serve: Ladle the *seviyan* into a serving bowl and decorate with silver *varq*.

159

MITHAI PLATTER

Preparation Time: 25 minutes
Cooking Time: 50 minutes + baking
Serves: 4-5

Radhicka Agarwal

Kalakand

Ingredients

Cottage cheese (*paneer*), mashed	100 g
Sweetened condensed milk	½ cup
Dried rose petals	⅓ cup
Sugar	⅓ cup
Betel (*paan*) leaves	
Saffron threads	7-8

Method

- Mash the *paneer* with a fork and mix in the condensed milk.

- Combine rose petals and sugar in a heavy-bottomed pan with 2 tablespoons water and cook on medium heat, stirring continuously, till it thickens to the consistency of jam.

- Dip the *paan* leaves in the sugar syrup made for *gujiya* (below).

- Heat an oven to 180°C/350°F/Gas 4.

- Spoon half the *paneer* mixture into a baking tray; arrange the sweetened *paan* leaves on top and spread the rose petal jam (*gulkand*) on top of the leaves. Spread the remaining *paneer* mixture over the *gulkand*. Sprinkle with saffron threads.

- Bake in the preheated oven for 15-20 minutes or till the top is a light golden brown.

- Remove, cool and refrigerate the *kalakand* for a while till set. Cut into squares.

Gujiya

Ingredients

Dough

Refined flour (*maida*)	150 g
Salt to taste	
Ghee	2 tbsp
Oil for deep-frying	

Stuffing

Khoya, grated	100 g
Finely chopped mixed dried fruit	3 tbsp
Grated rind of 2 tangerines	

Sugar Syrup

Sugar	½ cup
Water	½ cup
Magai paan leaves	2

To serve: Place a square of *kalakand* on a plate. Place a *gujiya* on top and garnish with *magai paan* leaves.

Method

- To make the dough, combine the flour, salt and ghee and knead to make a moderately stiff dough. Wrap in cling film and set aside to rest the dough for 15 minutes.

- For the stuffing, heat the *khoya* and cook for a few seconds. Mix in the dried fruit and orange rind, cook for a few minutes, remove and cool.

- Divide the dough into small portions and roll out into squares. Place a little stuffing in the centre of each square and bring the edges of the dough together to make a wonton.

- Heat the oil in a *kadai* and deep-fry the wontons till golden and crisp. Remove and drain on absorbent paper.

- For the sugar syrup, combine water and sugar and cook till it attains a one-string consistency. Dip the prepared wontons (*gujiya*) in the syrup, drain and set aside.

Baking Queen Radhicka made her mark in MasterChef Kitchen with this innovative twist on a traditional dish. She was the only contestant in the entire show to win the Golden Apron.

Spinach seems to be Jayanandan's lucky ingredient. He cooked spinach and banana for his MasterChef audition and was selected. In the Grand Finale, when he was competing against Pankaj for the coveted title of MasterChef India, he decided to cook a spinach dessert which impressed the judges because of the innovativeness of the dish.

SWEET CHEESY BASIL

Jayanandan Bhaskar

Preparation Time: 15 minutes
Cooking Time: 25-30 minutes
Serves: 12-16 kebabs

Ingredients

Spinach leaves	500 g
Fresh basil leaves	10 -15
Milk	5 tbsp
Mawa, grated	50 g
Caster sugar	100 g
Cinnamon powder	¼ tsp
Ricotta cheese	100 g
Cranberries, chopped	1 tbsp
Pistachios, chopped	1 tbsp

To decorate

Chopped cranberries and pistachios

Method

- In a pan, combine the spinach, basil and milk and cook for 2-3 minutes till the spinach softens but does not change colour.

- Purée the spinach mixture in a blender, making sure not to over process the mixture or the spinach will turn black.

- Heat the *mawa* in a frying pan till it softens and becomes moist. Mix in the caster sugar and spinach purée and cook for 1 minute. Add the cinnamon powder, ricotta, cranberries and pistachios and cook for 1 more minute.

To serve: Spoon the spinach into individual bowls and decorate with chopped cranberries and pistachios.

GLOSSARY

ENGLISH	HINDI	ENGLISH	HINDI
Almond	Badam	Indian salmon	Rawas
Aniseed	Saunf	Jaggery	Gur
Apricot	Khubani	Kidney beans	Rajma
Asafoetida	Hing	Leg of lamb or mutton	Raan
Asparagus	Shatwar	Mace	Javitri
Basil	Tulsi	Maize flour	Makai ka atta
Bay leaf	Tej patta	Milk, evaporated till semi-solid	Mawa/Khoya
Bengal gram	Kala chana	Minced Meat	Keema
Bengal gram flour	Besan	Mint	Pudina
Bengal gram, split	Chana dal	Musk melon	Kharbooj
Bengal gram, split and roasted	Daria dal	Mustard oil	Rai ka tel / Sarson ka tel
Betel leaf	Paan	Mustard seeds	Rai/Sarson
Black cardamoms	Badi elaichi	Nutmeg	Jaiphal
Black cumin	Shahi jeera	Olives	Jaitun
Black lentils, skinless, split	Dhuli urad dal	Onion seeds	Kalonji
Black lentils, split	Chilkewali urad dal	Orange	Narangi/ Santra
Black peppercorns	Kali mirch	Parsley	Ajmoda
Brinjal/ Aubergine/Eggplant	Baingan	Pear	Naspati
Broccoli	Hari phoolgobhi	Pine nuts	Chilgoza
Broken wheat	Dalia	Pineapple	Annanas
Browned onion	Bhuna pyaaz	Poppy seeds	Khus khus
Button mushrooms	Khumb	Prawns/shrimp	Jheenga
Capsicum	Shimla mirch	Puffed Bread	Puri/Luchi
Caraway seeds	Shia jeera/Vilayati jeera	Pure ghee	Desi ghee
Cardamom	Elaichi	Raisins	Kishmish
Carom seeds	Ajwain	Refined Flour	Maida
Cashew nuts	Kaju	Ridged gourd	Turai
Caster sugar	Pisi hui chini	Rose petal preserve	Gulkand
Cauliflower	Phoolgobhi	Rose water	Gulab jal
Chickpeas	Kabuli chana	Saffron	Kesar
Cinnamon	Dalchini	Sandalwood	Chandan
Cloves	Laung	Screw pine	Kewra
Coconut	Nariyal	Semolina	Rawa/Sooji
Coconut, dried	Khopra/Gari	Sesame seeds	Til
Coriander leaves	Hara dhania	Shallots	Chhote pyaaz
Coriander seeds	Dhania	Soda bicarbonate	Meetha soda
Corn kernels	Makai ke dane	Soup	Shorba
Cottage cheese	Paneer, Chhena	Spice	Masala
Cumin seeds	Jeera	Spinach	Palak
Curry leaves	Kadhi patta	Spring onion	Hara pyaaz
Dessert beans, dried	Sangri	Star anise	Chakri Phool/Badiyan
Dessert berries, dried	Ker	Sweet limes	Mosambi
Dill	Suva	Tamarind	Imli
Dried ginger powder	Sonth	Turmeric	Haldi
Dried mango powder	Amchur	Vermicelli	Seviyan
Edible silver foil	Chandi ka varq	Vetiver	Khus
Fennel seeds	Badi saunf	Vetiver roots	Khus ki jad
Fenugreek leaves, dried	Kasoori methi	Vinegar	Sirka
Fenugreek seeds	Methi dana	Walnuts	Akhrot
Flat bread	Chapati, Roti, Naan	Wholewheat flour	Atta
Fox nuts	Makhana	Wok	Kadai
Galangal	Paan ki jad	Yam	Jimikand
Griddle	Tawa	Yellow pumpkin	Kaddu
Honey	Shahad	Yoghurt	Dahi
		Yoghurt salad or sauce	Raita
		Yoghurt, drained (hung)	Chakka